MW00773246

Flannery O'Connor

Flannery O'Connor

WRITING A THEOLOGY
OF DISABLED HUMANITY

Timothy J. Basselin

BAYLOR UNIVERSITY PRESS

© 2013 by Baylor University Press
Waco, Texas 76798-7363

All Rights Reserved. No part of this publication may be reproduced,
stored in a retrieval system, or transmitted, in any form or by any
means, electronic, mechanical, photocopying, recording, or otherwise,
without the prior permission in writing of Baylor University Press.

Cover Design by Andrew Brozyna, AJB Design, Inc.
Cover Image courtesy of the Flannery O'Connor Collection, Georgia
    College and State University Library
Book Design by Diane Smith

Library of Congress Cataloging-in-Publication Data

Basselin, Timothy J.
 Flannery O'Connor : writing a theology of disabled humanity / Timothy J. Basselin.
  158 p. cm.
 Includes bibliographical references and index.
 ISBN 978-1-60258-765-6 (hardback : acid-free paper)
 1. O'Connor, Flannery—Criticism and interpretation. 2. O'Connor,
Flannery—Religion. 3. People with disabilities in literature. 4. Theology
in literature. 5. Christianity in literature. I. Title.
 PS3565.C57Z583 2013
 813'.54--dc23
                                    2012028957

Printed in the United States of America on acid-free paper with a mini-
mum of 30% post-consumer waste recycled content.

To my father

She saw the man's face twisted close to her own . . .

—"A Good Man Is Hard to Find"

Contents

Foreword

God is a mystery, and it is hard to know which of our efforts in life reach beyond to touch eternity and which will only return to dust. This book may well only be dust, but the process of its creation has surely had eternal consequences. The book's slow process of crafting has provided ample (perhaps too much) opportunity for many people in my life to care for and support me. Their love and encouragement have shaped my soul. They have invested in me because they believe in investing in people the way God has invested in humanity. Nothing has been requested in return. They have simply given, and from this I have learned what grace means.

Grace is gift, freely received but rarely free to give, for to give grace requires sacrifice. Those who have given me grace have sacrificed themselves for my sake over and over again. Foremost among the gracious in my life is my wife, Robin, who has given more of herself for me than I have for her. She has outgraced me in our first thirteen years of marriage, but I hope to catch up with her at some point in the next fifty years, years which I cannot imagine without her. She obviously learned how to give grace from her parents, who have sacrificed for our family innumerable times: helping us struggle through difficulty, helping us celebrate the good, caring for our children to give us time to work when needed. My mentor, Rob Johnston at Fuller Theological Seminary, and many friends have also been invaluable in listening to me and in gracing me with their insights and advice along the way as I wrestled with new perspectives.

The concepts found in this book were learned in my academic and personal journey. The underpinning tone of the book was taught to me without the use of words by my mother, Mary. At the age of forty she had the life she had desired. She was married to a wonderful husband and father, and they had two growing, active boys. She was a math teacher at a small Christian school which her boys attended, and the whole family was involved at church. She had grown up as the daughter of a preacher, and she now headed a program for the girls of the church and was married to a deacon of the church. Her faith in God was the most significant thing in her life, followed closely by her love for her family.

At the age of forty-one, her life was completely broken due to a severe head injury that my father received. After being in a coma for a few months and in the hospital for nearly a year, my father returned home a very different man. He could no longer ride motorcycles or skateboards with his boys, because he was in a wheelchair and his brain function was greatly compromised. He operated on the level of a first-grader instead of a middle-aged man who was a husband and a father. Additionally, complete amnesia had erased their entire life together. Seventeen years of the memories that make a relationship what it is were now gone, vanished like a wisp of smoke in a gentle breeze. Rather than having a partner in life and child-rearing, she now had to care for my father as one cares for a child. She had lost her spouse, and she was now a single parent to two boys who were becoming teenagers and had lost their father.

Many nights I remember hearing her sobbing in her room, and I knew she was on her knees crying out her prayers. "Why, God? Why?" I would hear her ask. Then as the weeping subsided, sometimes a half hour or a full hour later, "Not my will, Lord, not my will . . ." I am not sure who taught her how to accept the world's suffering and to keep believing, but I do know where I learned it. My suspicion is that she learned acceptance *as* she wrestled, the same as so many have before her, all the way back to Jacob. The floor of her bedroom was her schoolmaster, her tears her education. How else can one know the grace and formation that comes through suffering? Books cannot instill this mystery; they can only hint at it, glimpse it from a distance.

As I have come to appreciate O'Connor's work, I have done so in the light of my own experience (just as we all do). Early on I struggled to understand why I was so drawn to her, what made her work so profound to me. I came to realize my appreciation was tied to her ability to enflesh this mystery. Divine justice and divine grace were somehow revealed through the grotesque in her stories. I could not explain it, but somewhere deep within I knew that mystery's truth.

In my struggle to understand and put words to it, I was encouraged by my mentor, Rob Johnston, to seek out Amos Yong and to learn about disability studies. I immersed myself in the perspective that is disability studies, and I quickly began to see connections between O'Connor's disability and her uniqueness as a writer. In exploring a theology of disability, I began to develop a voice that could express some of the mystery I felt deep inside when I read O'Connor's fiction. The following book was written from the perspective I gained from disability studies, a theology of disability, and from my mother.

Mary Elizabeth (my mother) and Mary Flannery (O'Connor's given name) have a great deal in common, both being brilliant and faithful Christian women in the South. What truly sets them apart for me, though, in their commonality with one another is the grotesqueness of their lives and the grace with which they accepted the *whole* of life as a gift from God. Their sacrifices have been a gift to me, a grace I hope I can give others.

CHAPTER 1

The Face of the Good Is Grotesque, Too

Flannery O'Connor was diagnosed with lupus just as she became a professional writer, and she died fourteen years later at the young age of thirty-nine. Five years after diagnosis, she wrote curiously about her illness: "I have never been anywhere but sick. In a sense sickness is a place, more instructive than a long trip to Europe, and it's always a place where there's no company, where nobody can follow. Sickness before death is a very appropriate thing and I think those who don't have it miss one of God's mercies."[1]

O'Connor's words here are foreign to us.[2] Understanding sickness as "appropriate" and as "one of God's mercies" is antithetical to our cultural ideals of autonomy and self-sufficiency, as well as to our theologies of prosperity and even our understandings of the *imago Dei*. Her antagonism to our cultural ideals is consistent and is the most common theme in her writing. She is shouting at us, after all, critiquing any utopian visioning of modernity that would have imperfections eradicated in hopes of relieving society of its need for God. The profundity of O'Connor's writing is in precise contrast to these modern ideals as she enfleshes humanity's need for God within our imperfections, pointing us

1

to our common original sin. Her acceptance of illness, therefore, is the flip side of the coin that is her critique of modernity.

Of course, O'Connor's critics and admirers have all already recognized her drawings of large and startling figures as powerful critiques. What this study explores is O'Connor's use of illness, limitation, and human physical imperfection as sites for appropriate visitations from God. Modern culture's obsession with unflawed bodies rarely allows for speech about death or sickness, much less their being appropriate. Likewise, the proliferation of theologies focusing on health and wealth would find the idea of sickness-as-divinely-appropriate blasphemous. In our culture and our theologies, sickness and death engender fear and pity. In O'Connor's fiction, however, we find that grotesqueries are mysteriously transformed into loci for God's mercies.

In contrast to modernity's dealings with imperfections, in O'Connor's work God's mercy is never sentimental. God does not appear at the end of her stories and take pity on the poor souls she has crafted; mercy does not operate from the outside and relieve her characters. Rather, grace or the possibility for grace arrives only through the experience of grotesque limitations; mercy is forged in the fires of suffering. This burning vehicle for mercy in her stories also burns away her readers' sentimentality toward the characters. We do not pity the grandmother in "A Good Man Is Hard to Find," because her own hypocrisy and lies and limitations bring about her fate. The absence of sentimentality allows (or forces) O'Connor's readers to identify with her characters, and we realize that our sins mirror theirs. What draws us to her fiction, though, is a mystery that goes beyond this realization of sin—it is the mystery of how grace and mercy appear as though suddenly birthed out of the womb that has been the grandmother's sin and limitation. The slaughter of her family, her culpability in their deaths, and even the questioning of her own faith create the merciful realization of her kinship with the Misfit. "'She would of been a good woman,' The Misfit said, 'if it had been somebody there to shoot her every minute of her life.'"[3] The purpose of O'Connor's fiction is to hold such a gun to her reader, not to scare the hell out of him but to make him a good man. The mystery O'Connor engenders better than any other writer is not that a good man is hard to find, but that to find one takes hardness and difficulty. This mystery of grace-from-suffering, portrayed again and again in her fiction, resulted from the daily mercy that was her own sickness. To put it differently, O'Connor was a good woman because lupus was there every minute of her adult life. Lupus was her mercy, it was appropriate, because lupus fashioned the good within her. Such a mystery cannot be explained or understood, but can only be pushed into, lived, and expanded.

Early in her career, O'Connor did not perceive the full good in her writing. She, like her critics, primarily saw the mirror she raised to reflect modernity's grotesque sin. Late in her career, though, she began to see how "the face of the good is grotesque, too." Her profound realization began at a very specific time one day as she sat at home surrounded by nuns.

Mary Ann and the "New Perspective"

Mary Ann was grotesque. Born with a tumor on one side of her face, she arrived at Our Lady of Perpetual Help Home in Atlanta at the age of three and carried a certificate of death with a six-month prognosis. She had endured blood transfusions, radium, X-rays, and the removal of one of her eyes, but the tumor continued to grow. Her mother was young, also ill, had three other children, and could no longer care for her, so Mary Ann was transported from Louisville to Atlanta to live with the sisters at the home. The next nine years of her life proved a great blessing to her caregivers and anyone that visited Mary Ann, as is attested in a book the sisters wrote about her entitled *A Memoir of Mary Ann*, a book for which O'Connor wrote the introduction.

In June of 1961, three years before her death, O'Connor wrote in a letter to Betty Hester, "In the future, anybody who writes anything about me is going to have to read everything I have written in order to make legitimate criticism, even and particularly the Mary Ann piece."[4] Her claim is intriguing since her introduction to the book is not the forceful fiction that has established her as a preeminent American short story writer;

nor is it one of her famous essays that elucidates her vision as an artist. Nevertheless, O'Connor felt that this short reflection on a little girl whom she never even met held the key to any legitimate criticism of her work. At the end of the introduction, O'Connor reveals a "new perspective" on her own work that she has acquired.

In the introduction, O'Connor tells her reader that after the death of Mary Ann the sisters were so touched by her life that they sent O'Connor a letter asking her to write Mary Ann's life story. Upon opening the letter, O'Connor glanced at a photo of Mary Ann and quickly put it aside. Finishing the letter, O'Connor determined she was not the person to write the story, and she picked up the photograph "to give it a last cursory look before returning it to the Sisters. It showed a little girl in her First Communion dress and veil. . . . Her small face was straight and bright on one side. The other side was protuberant, the eye was bandaged, and the nose and mouth crowded slightly out of place."[5] O'Connor's reply suggested that the sisters write the memoir, and she could write an introduction.

Once the memoir was written, the sisters visited O'Connor at Andalusia to discuss the manuscript. Having read some of O'Connor's stories, one of the sisters asked why she wrote about such grotesque characters, why the grotesque of all things was her vocation. O'Connor recounts, "I was struggling to get off the hook she had me on when another of our guests supplied the one answer that would make it immediately plain to all of them. 'It's your vocation, too.' "[6]

The statement that O'Connor's vocation was the same as the sisters' was an enlightening one for the sisters—and for O'Connor. O'Connor notes, "This opened up for me also a new perspective on the grotesque. Most of us have learned to be dispassionate about evil, to look it in the face and find, as often as not, our own grinning reflections with which we do not argue." O'Connor's words here can act as a summary for how her fiction generally gets interpreted, indeed how she interpreted much of her work for the majority of her life. The physical grotesques in her fiction are metaphorical mirrors for the characters' (and readers') moral grotesques. She thus characterizes her work as drawing "large and startling" figures on the outside to wake us up to the immensity of our shared original sin.

As O'Connor continues her explanation, however, she provides the new perspective, "but good is another matter. Few have stared at that long enough to accept the fact that its face too is grotesque, that in us the good is something under construction. The modes of evil usually receive worthy expression. The modes of good have to be satisfied with a cliché or a smoothing-down that will soften their real look." O'Connor does not say the grotesque can be good. She does not offer the reader a pastoral platitude that God can use evil as a tool to work all things together for good. Good is not outside of the grotesque waiting to be bestowed. Instead, she says the face of the good *is* grotesque. She continues, "When we look into the face of good, we are liable to see a face like Mary Ann's, full of promise."[7] That is, the face of the good may well be misshapen and half eaten away by a cancerous tumor that carries with it a death sentence. The face of the good may be O'Connor's own lupus. Or, put in larger theological terms, the face of redemption is God crucified on a Roman cross.

To be clear, the argument here is not that O'Connor presents a shifted philosophical perspective in which bad is good and good is bad. She does not encourage a trick of the mind where if we simply think about things differently, we will be able to find beauty in them. She instead prophesies against our need to fix everything and tells us our falsely perfected world leaves no room for the mysterious activity of God. We suffer from a lack of recognizing and experiencing God's presence within broken humanity. The answer is not to change one's perspective about the meaning of life's circumstances as good or bad, but to change one's perspective about life in a broader sense—to understand that life is a good gift to be accepted, struggles and all.

The Good Friday cross that seems desperately abandoned by all things good awaits the disciples' response. Even with Christ's repeated warnings and exhortations that the Son of Man must die to be raised again, they experience a failure of imagination.

They cannot comprehend the greatest good being accomplished on a cross. No teaching, not even Christ's instructions and example, can prepare them to discern the authentic good from evil. Though they cannot imagine any of it is true, they are called to believe, accepting what has been given and waiting within the unknown. In this waiting, in this mystery, faith forms. O'Connor wrote that evil is not a problem to be fixed but "a mystery to be endured."[8] Acceptance of life as given, even those aspects of life that culture labels grotesque, is central to her work, and is so because it was central to her acceptance of the mystery of her disability.

What the nuns lived out on a daily basis in their care for Mary Ann and others with diagnoses of terminal cancer became O'Connor's new perspective on her fiction. Nurturing those things "full of promise" was the significance of the work of the sisters, of their vocation of the grotesque. Because of their close relation with the ill children, they broke the cultural and seemingly necessary ties between the grotesque and evil. Their work proclaimed that the greatest good can be found in the center of what society has labeled evil, in the midst of great and innocent suffering. Both vocations, that of the sisters and O'Connor's writing, displace the cultural and ideological definitions of good and evil with lived embodiments of authentic good and evil. O'Connor's ability to recognize this mystery came not only from her genius as a writer, but primarily through her own lived limitations.

The new perspective O'Connor describes provides tremendous insight for understanding her work, but has been little understood. Her stories continually point out that because society has wrongly identified the good, the face of the authentic good gets "satisfied with a cliché or a smoothing-down." The good country characters in O'Connor's fiction, such as the grandmother, are full of these clichés, at least until the weight and violence of O'Connor's stories crumble the facade of their culturally defined goods. The obvious aftermath of these stories is the revelation of the true evils of original sin upon which cultural goods are built.

But the power and meaning of the stories lies in the mystery of a mercy that lingers beyond the last period of the last sentence.

As we see when she admits to setting Mary Ann's picture quickly aside, O'Connor was also affected by social constructs of beauty and the good. Yet, since she was an unwed, disabled woman in the South, she also understood what it was to be quickly set aside by society, and her own marginality helped her recognize that the true residence of evil had been misplaced. The fact that O'Connor's new perspective on the grotesque—this key for critics to understand her work—was realized in reference to another person who died young from a disability, yet lived a spectacular life, is no mere coincidence.

Certainly O'Connor's denial that her illness had any effect on her writing is in no small part responsible for the lack of attention her illness has generated. Her denial, though, was aimed at the presumption of any pity that may have led others to sentimentalize her life, or worse, her fiction. Though she downplayed the illness' effect, she also regularly credited the circumstances of her life, particularly those created by the lupus—as well as the lupus itself—for making her writing better. She touted her move and confinement to Georgia as the best thing that could have happened to her writing. Denying culture's sentimental pity for her loss of independence, she stated the sickness was a "blessing in disguise."[9]

Popular wisdom suggests that a writer should be out experiencing the entire world in order to write about it, which was also O'Connor's view before contracting lupus. When diagnosed, she had recently lived at the Writers' Workshop at the University of Iowa, at an artist colony in Yaddo, New York, and in an apartment in New York City, and was currently living with Robert and Sally Fitzgerald in Connecticut. At this point in her life, she was certain that being confined to rural Georgia would entail the end of her creativity, her vocation. She rather quickly found, however, that the best of her work would be done there. The unthinkable and socially grotesque, her disease and her return to Georgia, allowed her to focus and to truly enter her "country."

Disability's Effect on O'Connor

*To call yourself a Georgia writer is certainly to declare a limita-
tion, but one which, like all limitations, is a gateway to reality.*

—Mary Flannery O'Connor, "The Regional Writer"

Mary Flannery O'Connor, her full given name, was grotesque.
Throughout her writing career her body was ravaged by disease,
and her life was defined by many other limitations. Western-
influenced societies teach youth that whatever is imagined or
dreamed can be accomplished through hard work. Dreams and
desires, in fact, are proclaimed as the gateways to reality. In particular, the American Dream imagines the pursuit of happiness
by an autonomous individual who is self-sufficient and unfettered by limits. In contrast, O'Connor considered her limitations
gateways to reality. Her claim renounces Enlightenment ways
of thinking and constructs an alternative vision of how to be
in the world. Disability, especially when understood theologically, helps imagine alternative visions of being that are dependent on limitation and mutual vulnerability. An exploration of
O'Connor's view of limitation, in particular how her view is
connected to her disability, reveals that an acceptance of limitation is fundamental to her challenge to modernity, a challenge
that became the foundation of her fiction.

O'Connor's life and stories regularly broke down the social
constructs of what is "normal." Uninterested in social conventions, and thus rarely ever mistaken for being normal, O'Connor
was instead well known for her appreciation for and pursuit of
the atypical, even the bizarre. At the age of five she had already
become famous for one such oddity. A news agency came to
her home in Savannah and filmed a story about her backwards-
walking chicken.[10] The story then ran before movies around the
country. She claimed the event "marked me for life."[11]

In her autobiographical essay "The King of the Birds" she
explains how she began to collect chickens as a child: "What
had been only a mild interest became a passion, a quest. I had
to have more and more chickens. I favored those with one green

eye and one orange or with overlong necks and crooked combs. I wanted one with three legs or three wings but nothing in that line turned up."[12] She later became entranced by the oddity, splendor, and mystery of peacocks. At the time she wrote "The King of the Birds" she had over forty of these striking peafowl at her farm Andalusia.

O'Connor's eccentricity went well beyond her birds and the farm they all lived on together; her iconoclasm was plain to most with whom she came into contact. She was known for enjoying "Coca-Colas laced with black coffee" and for putting "sharp cheese on her oatmeal,"[13] trivial matters to be sure, but biographical accounts of her overflow with similar idiosyncrasies, as do her letters. Being a normal southern belle, as many in her family and her town hoped she would, was not simply unthinkable for her but was purposefully fought against. One has only to glance over the cartoons she drew for the school newspaper while in college to recognize her sarcastic view of proper southern belle behavior.[14] O'Connor always reveled in turning social conventions on their head. While in high school, Margaret Abercrombie's home economics class required the girls to sew an outfit. All the other girls sewed Sunday dresses for themselves. However, as a fellow student reported, "On the appointed day Flannery arrived with her pet duckling, and a whole outfit of underwear and clothes, beautifully sewn to fit the duck!"[15]

Both in her life and her writings, O'Connor attempted to change the social perception that deviation from the norm is shocking or morally deviant. O'Connor understood that the social ideal of a "perfect" person is an ideal of which everyone necessarily falls short and an ideal toward which none should be striving. Indeed, the attempt to gain perfection is what should be considered morally deviant. O'Connor had no problem being imperfect according to societal standards. Her fiction not only embraces abnormality, or the grotesque, as it is named in literary terms, but uses abnormality and society's shock at the grotesque to reveal the truth of the human condition.

For a society that worships limitlessness, limits constitute a roadblock. O'Connor's profound personal limitations set her apart as a near-hopeless case for the idealisms of modernity. She was unmarried in the South; she was a Catholic in the South; she was a woman in the South; and to complicate all of these, she was a female intellectual in the 1950s and 1960s . . . in the South. The social circles in Milledgeville that would accept such a person were not many; often the social circle of her own dining room table questioned her motives. These social boundaries, though, were not her greatest limitation. Her greatest limitation both socially and physically was her disability.[16]

O'Connor's writings, particularly from the last five years of her life, reveal not only that she lived with limitation, but that she thought consistently about its significance. O'Connor wrote, "I believe that the basic experience of everyone is the experience of human limitation."[17] When the characters in her stories ignore the truth of what limits them is often when they begin to be overtaken by evil. Yet she did not view limitations, as modern culture views them, simply as challenges we must find ways to get around or to overcome, road blocks to be burst through or stepping stones toward an alternate route to perfection. For O'Connor, that which holds us back is that which defines our humanity: our limitations become the face of the good. O'Connor noted, "Fiction is the most impure and the most modest and the most human of the arts. It is closest to man in his sin and his suffering and his hope. . . . We are limited human beings, and the novel is a product of our best limitations."[18] Again, her perspective is countercultural. We are accustomed to thinking of the production of great art as the result of that which is best about us, an overcoming of obstacles, a reaching toward limitlessness. For O'Connor art may well be what is best about us, but the route to the good lies through limitation, not despite it.

In O'Connor's thought and work the theological is always close at hand, so she relates the significance of limitation and art to the incarnation—God as a limited human being. Giving advice to young writers, she references fiction as being "so very much an incarnational art," and then claims, "The fact is that the materials of the fiction writer are the humblest. Fiction is about everything human and we are made out of dust, and if you scorn getting yourself dusty, then you shouldn't try to write fiction. It's not a grand enough job for you."[19] Putting off for now the theological implications and import of calling fiction an "incarnational art," the irony of the incarnation not being a grand enough job for the young writer should not be lost. The incarnation reference serves to create an analogy between the lofty goals of art and the lofty goals of God's redemption of the world. Yet both goals are achieved through the humble and "dusty" means of enfleshing a very limited humanity, not by escaping such limitation or saving humanity from its limitation or even finding ways to overcome limitation, but simply by being limited.

O'Connor's perspective on limitation pervades her work because she was busy prophetically challenging the arrogant philosophies of modernity that assume attainable perfection. In an essay entitled "The Teaching of Literature," she writes that a "sense of loss is natural to us, and it is only in these centuries when we are afflicted with the doctrine of the perfectibility of human nature by its own efforts that the vision of the freak in fiction is so disturbing."[20] For O'Connor, limitation and loss are normal or natural; the modern doctrine of perfectibility is what is freakishly removed from reality. She therefore considered the freaks, with whom her fiction is well littered, to represent the normal state of us all, and she calls her readers to recognize a new definition of normal.

Physical Diminishments

As noted, few have explored the significance limitation and disability played in O'Connor's thought and her fiction despite the fact that she wrote about limitation and limitation defined her life in so many ways. O'Connor perceived her "passive diminishments" as "gateways to reality," and just as with Mary Ann, O'Connor's physical limitations became the raw materials for fashioning her death in Christ.[21] O'Connor's understanding of limitation, though, was no mere philosophical exercise. She experienced limitation in very personal ways, both because of her lupus and as a writer. Concerning her vocation, she claims, "It has been my experience that in the process of making a novel, the serious novelist faces, in the most extreme way, his own limitations."[22] The experience of limitation is certainly true in relation to a poverty of words the writer may experience,[23] but O'Connor meant something more as well. She is writing about making limitations real, incarnating them in fiction. Incarnating limitations makes our creatureliness real—faces it, allows the reader to see it, and helps the reader to accept it. When the reader comes to terms with her limitations, she finds limitations are not necessarily something to be denounced. Rather, her acceptance frees her to walk through a gateway. Realizing our true reality of dependency was the goal of much of O'Connor's writing.

For O'Connor, facing "in the most extreme way" her own limitations at least partially meant facing her physical limitations. Lupus caused her greatest physical diminishments and became her greatest gateway to reality.[24] Lupus is a chronic autoimmune disease: it confuses a person's immune system, causing it to attack healthy tissues instead of attacking only viruses, bacteria, and germs. Once the immune system is confused it can attack any part of the body. Common symptoms include hair loss, extreme fatigue, photosensitivity, fevers, anemia, weight loss, joint pain, and loss of appetite. O'Connor experienced all of these symptoms and many others over the course of fourteen years, including many side effects due to experimental medicines, yet there is little evidence in her letters or in reports from friends concerning the pain she suffered. When she does mention her health, she wittily disguises or makes light of the disease's effect on her. In a letter to Caroline Gordon Tate in 1957, seven years after her diagnosis, she wrote, "I have lately been getting dizzy because I am taking a new medicine and have got an overdose of it. So I figure I'll do my staggering around at home. It takes some time for the dose to get regulated. Every time something new is invented, I get in on the ground floor with it."[25] Another example comes from a letter written in 1964, the year she died, in which she wrote a friend about her current stay in the hospital. "I am still here—into the third week. I had a transfusion Sareday &

another Sunday. . . . I don't know if I'm making progress or if there's any to be made. Let's hope they are learning something anyhow."[26]

O'Connor's humor masks the pain and fatigue with which she lived on a daily basis. Her disease regularly put her on crutches for months at a time and into hospitals for extended stays. She was also affected psychologically because she was well aware of the disease's end.[27] As mentioned, lupus also deprived her of strength and energy, particularly in the afternoons.[28] In addition to the symptoms of the disease itself, she constantly dealt with the side effects of medicines, in particular the steroids that were used to treat lupus in the 1950s. In a letter to Sally and Robert Fitzgerald in 1951, only a year after her diagnosis, she wrote, "the large doses of ATCH [hormones] send you off in a rocket and are scarcely less disagreeable than the disease."[29]

In the last five years of her life, O'Connor began to reference the disease in her letters more frequently. In 1959, she wrote to Cecil Dawkins, "The sun is greatly restricting my activities right now and will continue to do so, I'm afraid. The doctor says I can't go out of the house without stockings, gloves, long sleeves and large hat. (Sunlight influences lupus and causes joint symptoms). The spectacle of me in this get-up all summer is depressing to my imagination. We are having green glass put in the car."[30] Again, her wit nearly masks the disease's effect on her, but it does not take much reading between the lines to realize the great limitations that being restricted from going outside would have upon her.

From one perspective, certainly the one O'Connor preferred, her disability had nothing to do with her writing. She wrote characteristically in a letter, "My lupus has no business in literary considerations."[31] In another she wrote, "The disease is of no consequence to my writing since for that I use my head and not my feet."[32] Apart from her claims, though, the dearth of O'Connor scholarship interested in her disability gives one the impression that her disease had little, if any, effect on her fiction. All other aspects of her life—her Southern heritage and surroundings, her relationship with her mother, her gender and education—have been scrutinized and mined for relevance to the meaning of her work. Yet, her disability and its constant effects on her physically, mentally, and even on her locale have been largely ignored.

The relative silence concerning O'Connor's lupus may stem from society's unease with disability itself.[33] Enlightenment-influenced minds tend to ignore limitations or consider them as nothing more than obstacles to accomplishment. In evolutionary thinking, limitations are problems to be solved, and those of us encountering them are uncomfortable until we have figured out a solution. Disability, however, with its on-the-surface limitation, makes limitation undeniable. And when a person is the problem to be solved, we are uneasy and often quiet. We as a society still are not sure what to do with the disabled, still are not sure if they are whole people or if they need to be fixed first. Pointing out society's unease with disability is significant because a direct correlation exists between the meaning of O'Connor's work and how our culture perceives disability.[34] O'Connor's fiction challenges these assumptions about the disabled as well as our deeper philosophical assumptions about limitation in general. The heart of O'Connor's critique of modern culture is that she understands we cannot save ourselves, and she declares to us that we must realize our inability (our limitation) before we can be open to a saving force outside ourselves. Because O'Connor believed so powerfully in the reality of salvation, incarnations of limitation—whether they be real, such as lupus and the gas chambers of World War II, or fictional, such as those in her stories—were not faces of humanity half eaten away by disease and evil. They were instead faces half full of promise.

If O'Connor had referenced her disability more in her letters, and particularly if she had complained about it more, surely there would be a plethora of scholarship devoted to lupus' effects on her. Scholars could, from a place of sentimentality and pity, theorize about how difficult the disease was for her and how the freaks in her stories are her outlet for channeling her pain. O'Connor's letters and fiction, though, do not allow for sentimentality. She instead portrays acceptance of limitations, an acceptance that has confounded scholars. For our Enlightened society, to embrace disease and limitation is to turn on and attack our cultural ideals: a philosophical lupus.

Disability's Effect on O'Connor's Worldview and Writing

O'Connor's disability affected her writing in at least three ways: it caused her to move back to the South where she embraced being a Southern writer; it caused her to concentrate on her writing since it took all her strength away for doing anything else; and most importantly it allowed her to embody one of the most central elements of her faith—Christ's suffering. Admittedly, the first two are circumstantial. Possibly she would have been nearly as regional in her writing if she had remained in Connecticut with the Fitzgeralds, where she was when the lupus called her back home to Georgia. Also, she was known for her disciplined writing even before she was exiled to the Southern countryside and to having the strength to write only in the mornings. Nevertheless, the limitations of place (the South and a rural farm) and physicality (lack of strength and mobility) that lupus placed on her at least aided in her development in becoming a great regional writer. The force of the argument here, though, will be on the third point, that O'Connor's disability aided her in developing a keen sense of how limitations and even suffering must be accepted and embraced as participation in God's redemption of the world.

The following argument does not claim that in the overall scheme of things O'Connor's lupus ended up making her a better writer and that lupus' benefits somehow justify the pain with which she lived. The lupus did not make her a better writer, turn her into a saint, or give her any special insights. Disability as a means to an end is precisely the kind of sentimentality O'Connor wished to avoid when claiming the lupus had no effect on her writing. Lupus certainly did, however, change her life, most profoundly in cutting it short. What made her a better writer and gave her great insight was not the lupus itself but how she responded to the lupus and its death sentence. Her acceptance, not of the disease per se, but of life as given, as a gift, made all things, including "passive diminishments," meaningful to her calling and thereby good.

The first way lupus affected O'Connor is that she needed someone to help care for her and was forced to move in with her mother and thereby to return to the South. Her style was already Southern gothic when she lived at the Iowa Writers' Workshop and in New York at the Yaddo artist community and with Robert and Sally Fitzgerald in Connecticut, but there is no questioning that her move back to Andalusia, her family's farm in Milledgeville, helped her become one of the greatest regional writers the United States has known. Before the move could have a positive effect on her writing, though, she had to accept the change.[35]

Six years after her return, she wrote about accepting the change to a friend who was complaining about having to return to the South: "So it may be the South! You get no condolences from me. This is a Return I have faced and when I faced it I was roped and tied and resigned the way it is necessary to be resigned to death, and largely because I thought it would be the end of any creation, any writing, any WORK from me. And as I told you by the fence, it was only the beginning."[36] In another letter she discloses a similar thought: "It is perhaps good and necessary to get away from it [the South] physically for a while, but this is by no means to escape it. I stayed away from the time I was 20 until I was 25 with the notion that the life of my writing depended on my staying away. I would certainly have persisted in that delusion had I not got very ill and had to come home. The best of my writing has been done here."[37] Though slowly at first, she began to accept her return and realized the limitation of her locale as a gift to her. She too had thought she must be liberated from the limitations of her childhood in order to fly free as an artist and a person, but the lupus helped her understand that it was precisely her limitations that could help her and her writing break through to reality.

The farm, her family, the townspeople, the nearby asylum, and so much more of her locale became inspiration for her stories. A trip to Andalusia makes tangible the scenes her readers have imagined: Shiftlet walking up the long dirt driveway to the farm in "The Life You Save May Be Your Own"; the young girl moving from one upstairs bedroom to another to watch the boys coming to the farm in "A Circle in the Fire"; descriptions of the help's living quarters and of the tree lines in the distance in any of her stories. Biographies of O'Connor provide example after example of how she drew from her surroundings to create her stories, whether nearby railroad tracks, stories in the local paper, or her family members. O'Connor studied the details of landscapes and people alike, and her intense scrutiny of Andalusia and Milledgeville provided her the means for enfleshing her characters.

One further example of her fully coming to accept her "Return" is found in a letter she wrote after her single trip abroad. During the trip, she was plagued by a severe cold that lasted most of the seventeen-day journey. The comforts of home proved a welcome change. Shortly after returning to Andalusia, she wrote, "We went to Europe and I lived through it but my capacity for staying at home has now been perfected & is going to last me the rest of my life."[38]

Another way the lupus affected her writing was that it helped her focus. The rural location of the farm is partially responsible, but her focus on writing is also due to the weariness and immobility the disease created. In one letter she wrote, "I myself am afflicted with time, as I do not work out [of the house] on account of an energy-depriving ailment and my work in, being creative, can go on only a few hours a day. I live on a farm and don't see many people."[39] In another letter, after two years of living on the farm, she wrote to her mentor, Robert Lowell, at the Iowa Writers' Workshop, revealing both an early acceptance of her disease and new location and the benefit that attended: "I am making out fine in spite of any conflicting stories. . . . I have enough energy to write with and as that is all I have any business doing anyhow, I can with one eye squinted take it all as a blessing. What you have to measure out, you come to observe closer, or so I tell myself."[40] A few years later in another letter, she wrote, "I have had some bone trouble and for the last two years have been walking on crutches; I expect to be on them for two or three years more or longer—but when you can't be too active physically, there is nothing left to do but write so I may have a blessing in disguise."[41] Again, one cannot read these quotes without being struck by how countercultural they are in finding the disease that eventually killed her to be a blessing. Her take-it-as-a-blessing perspective runs from the beginning of her exile to the end of her life. In 1964 when she was restricted to a hospital bed and not even allowed visitors, she wrote, "I'm pleased I can't have company because it means what energy I've got I can use for my own bidnis, getting this book out. I've got to get it out before I get worse & should I get better I'll have other & new stuff to work on."[42] Unfortunately, she did not have a chance to work on anything else.

Along with concentrating on her art, her isolation and exhaustion allowed for our greatest insight into her personality: her letters. In one of her early letters, she wrote Father McCown, "I never mind writing anybody. In fact it is about my only way of visiting with people as I don't get around much and people seldom come to see us in the country."[43] The O'Connors only installed a telephone at the farm late in Flannery's life, so her primary means of communication was letters. Her hundreds of letters have been invaluable in helping her fans understand her, and they continue to be as new letters are discovered and released. In addition to maintaining friendships, her letters discuss everything from the terms of her contracts to what magazines and books she was reading to responses to school children confused about her stories. She responded to young authors who wrote her looking for encouragement, and she asked for advice from friends on the stories she was working on at the time.[44] Had she lived somewhere else and had easier access to friends, colleagues, or even a phone, we would not likely have the same wealth of insight her letters provide. Again, the argument here is not that the ends justify the means, that we should view her lupus positively because she wrote better stories and more letters due to living at Andalusia and having little energy for travel. Rather, the point is that lupus did in fact affect her life, and her acceptance of and response to the effects of lupus allowed her to become one of the greatest authors and personalities in American history.

Most significant, though, is a third way lupus affected O'Connor's writing: it caused her to live the reality of pain and suffering. As noted, it is easy to miss O'Connor's pain, even in her letters.[45] Reading between the lines, though, the difficulty of lupus becomes clear. She often referred to new medicines and their side effects, though she let on little as to the suffering they caused. She also lay in the hospital for weeks and months at a time. She had to turn down speaking engagements and invites to visit friends, and she was only able to write for a few hours each day. Yet O'Connor found a way to embrace these limitations. She wrote in a letter, "As far as I'm concerned, as long as I can get at that typewriter, I have enough. They expect me to improve or so they say. I expect anything that happens."[46] This quote, perhaps her strongest statement of acceptance, was written only a few months before the "anything" that was her death. At least part of the reason there are dead bodies in O'Connor's fiction is due to the looming presence of lupus in her life. In light of her watching her father die of the disease and her own stream of passive diminishments, O'Connor's acceptance of lupus is remarkable. Her acceptance, however, is not a resignation to a sad fate. Rather, it is an active acceptance of God's will and a prophetic challenge to the cultural insistence that such a fate is sad.

The insistence that her fate and the fates of others who are disabled or diseased are sad comes from prioritizing the extermination of suffering over the appreciation of mystery. Modern philosophies are not only uncomfortable with mystery, they have often proclaimed its extinction. O'Connor's challenge to a mystery-less modernity has been considered the essence of her fiction.[47] How her challenge to modernity was affected by her disability, though, has yet to be explored.

Fighting the Demons of Modernism

Of course, for modern society, imperfection *is* a sad and unacceptable fate. Therefore, persons with disabilities often receive the same sentimental treatment from society that O'Connor received from an old lady while on a shopping trip. Afterwards she wrote Betty Hester with this account:

> I have decided I must be a pretty pathetic sight with these crutches. I was in Atlanta the other day in Davison's. An old lady got on the elevator behind me and as soon as I turned around she fixed me with a moist gleaming eye and said in a loud voice, "Bless you, darling!" I felt exactly like the Misfit and I gave her a weakly lethal look, whereupon greatly encouraged, she grabbed my arm and whispered (very loud) in my ear. "Remember what they said to John at the gate darling!" It was not my floor, but I got off and I suppose the old lady was astounded at how quick I could get away on crutches. I have a one-legged friend and I asked her what they said to John at the gate. She said she reckoned they said, "the lame shall enter first." This may be because the lame will be able to knock everybody else down with their crutches.[48]

O'Connor's account of the elevator ride references many of the social (as opposed to only physical) realities of disability. The social weight of disability is evident in the first line. Whether or not O'Connor is pathetic is beside the point, because she is a "pathetic sight" to others. Our society assumes a great deal about the disabled. O'Connor's reaction to the lady resists the social stigma of disability, a stigma that totalizes a person according to a disability. The old lady tears up with presumptions about the miserable state of affairs in which O'Connor must be living. She assumes a certain sad state of non-ability that goes beyond the obvious limitation to walking and includes O'Connor's hearing. She thus speaks very loudly to O'Connor and then "whisper[s] (very loud)" in her ear. Unfortunately, being the recipients of misguided accommodations is a regular occurrence for the disabled. When the able-bodied, or temporarily able-bodied, see a disability, they often become socially uncomfortable with the person, not knowing what other parts of the person do not work.

In resisting the social stigma that accompanies disability, O'Connor turns a sign of disability, her crutches, into a helpful aid. She is able to get out of the elevator very quickly, surprising the old lady, and she imagines the lame enjoying an enhanced ability to muscle their way through to the front of the line to enter heaven. The disability thus becomes an agent for change, in this case allowing for creative maneuvering, which suggests that limitation can be good and useful.

Most significantly, though, O'Connor does not participate in the sentimentality the lady offers. The old lady is actually correct in presuming a difficult state of affairs for O'Connor. O'Connor's problem with her, though, is that the lady responds with sentiment. The lady does not seek to participate in O'Connor's suffering by truly helping in any vulnerable way. Instead, the lady's sentiment presumes that she and O'Connor are different, that the old lady is whole while O'Connor is broken. The lady's view is from above, looking down upon O'Connor. The sentiment also presumes that brokenness is pitiable, rather than natural. O'Connor refuses such sentimentality and exits with haste. Well-intentioned words from an old lady are not something one usually feels the need to escape, yet O'Connor is so opposed to them that she exits on the wrong floor. Her need for escape proves telling. The old woman, of course, is not the danger. Rather, O'Connor is escaping a particular philosophical viewpoint, as though it were a temptation or evil one must flee.

O'Connor's essay "The Church and the Fiction Writer" provides insight into her need to escape. In discussing how "fiction can transcend its limitations only by staying within them,"[49] O'Connor notes the average Catholic reader's preference for sentimentality, a Manichean preference that separates the physical from the spiritual:

By separating nature and grace as much as possible, he has reduced his conception of the supernatural to pious cliché and has become able to recognize nature in literature in only two forms, the sentimental and the obscene. . . . but the similarity between the two generally escapes him. He forgets that sentimentality is an excess, a distortion of sentiment usually in the direction of an overemphasis on innocence, and that innocence, whenever it is overemphasized in the ordinary human condition, tends by some natural law to become its opposite. We lost our innocence in the Fall, and our return to it is through the Redemption which was brought about by Christ's death and by our slow participation in it. Sentimentality is a skipping of this process in its concrete reality and an early arrival at a mock state of innocence.[50]

O'Connor fled the presumption of innocence that resided within the old lady's "Bless you, darling!" because she knew that such sentimentality skips the necessary, slow participation in Christ's death. She understood that she was indeed more likely to enter heaven's gates first by using her crutches as weapons than by relying on such sentimentality. Furthermore, O'Connor believed this woman's sentimentality revealed the primary problem with modernity: the refusal of the realities of the fall and an attempt to bypass Christ's death by employing our own means of salvation. Like the lady placing O'Connor at heaven's gate without knowing anything about her, modernity attempts to skip the concrete reality of suffering and presumes a mock state of innocence, presumes the perfectibility of humanity by its own efforts. The old lady's sentimentality belies her participation in this modern philosophy, which O'Connor saw as the great evil of her time and therefore felt she must flee as quickly as possible. She believed that what one does not accept (another person's sentimentality) is as significant as what one does accept. For O'Connor, participation in Christ's suffering, which is the root of much of the violence in her fiction, was the only means of return to our redemption. Indeed, violence and death are sometimes the only means of return for a society that has so perfected mock innocence.

Our society continues to oscillate between pitying the misfortune of the disabled and fearing the disabled as embodiments of chaos.[51] Religious views of disability have differed very little. Christians throughout the ages have perceived disability as an extreme. The disabled are "either divinely blessed or damned: the defiled evildoer or the spiritual superhero."[52] The view of disability in churches usually leans toward the spiritual super-hero, or in O'Connor's words an "overemphasis on innocence." This results in what have been termed "folk theodicies," which come across to disabled persons in the form of well-meaning clichés such as "'You are special in God's eyes. That's why you were given this disability'; 'Don't worry about your pain and suffering now, in heaven you will be made whole'; and 'Thank God, it isn't worse.' "[53] Certainly one of these folk theodicies was in the old lady's mind when she grabbed O'Connor's arm and whispered loudly in her ear.

O'Connor considered the cultural pervasiveness of senti-mentality terribly dangerous, especially its development within the church. Such sentimentality participates in the larger cul-tural problems of self-sufficient autonomy. The folk theodicy comments that the disabled have received from churchgoers assume an unrealistically "perfect" body and mind as normal. Deviation from the norm calls forth the viewer's sentimentality, which springs from a philosophical stance that takes for granted humanity's need to, and ability to, eradicate suffering. Once again, modern philosophy leaves no room for mystery.

In contrast to folk theodicies, O'Connor understood that disability does not automatically develop character and allow the "lame" to enter heaven first. Entering heaven only occurs by the slow participation in Christ's death, no matter who the person is. One of O'Connor's purposes in her fiction is to com-municate that to avoid suffering may well be to avoid God's work in the world. Suffering, though, does not realize mystery on its own. The mystery lies in acceptance.

O'Connor traced the problem to the Enlightenment.[54] The Enlightenment championed reason and answers over spiritual-ity and mystery, eventually reducing reality to the malleable and thus conquerable state of physical material. O'Connor wrote,

"Since the eighteenth century, the popular spirit of each suc-
ceeding age has tended more and more to the view that the
ills and mysteries of life will eventually fall before the scientific
advances of man, a belief that is still going strong even though
this is the first generation to face total extinction because of
these advances."[55] The modern perspective, believing it can
conquer all ills and mysteries, displaces any need for help. The
Enlightenment denies vulnerability, and thus denies the true
state of humanity, and the old lady in the elevator participated
by mistaking inability and vulnerability for abnormality.

Ultimately, the lady's modern-influenced philosophy is
gnostic. Enlightenment thinkers such as the philosophers "Descartes, Rousseau, Kant, and Hegel, and after them, romantic
and modern artists [perpetuated] two essentially gnostic ideas
Americans have made their own: (1) that the imagination can
be made pure and free, unfettered by the body and (2) that the
self can birth itself in complete freedom and independence from
the authority and determination of others."[56] The first of these
gnostic ideas, that the imagination can be made pure, has led to
the dominance of reason as the center of what it means to be
human. Descartes' famous dictum *cogito ergo sum* determined
that only reason can be trusted as the foundation of being.[57]
The prioritizing of thinking set up for the Enlightenment and
following centuries of Western thought a dualism between the
higher functions of reason and the lower functions of all things
physical. According to the light of the Enlightenment, all problems can be conquered once their causes are understood and
the imagination is allowed the freedom necessary to formulate
a solution. The body operates as little more than a vessel for the
tremendous powers of the mind. Sentimentality participates in
this gnostic version of reality because it denies the mysteries of
the body, specifically suffering, which it views only as a physical
problem that must be solved by triumphs of the mind. In distinct contrast, O'Connor understood suffering as a mysterious
ingredient of life, a life fully given by the Creator.

The second gnostic concept, that the self can achieve complete freedom and independence from the authority of others, has become the American-perfected ideal of self-sufficient autonomy. O'Connor described her first collection of short stories, *A Good Man Is Hard to Find*, as "nine stories about original sin" before the tenth was added.[58] In them, and in all of her work, she attempts to reveal the original sin with which all humanity is born and which the Enlightenment has championed: believing we are the creators of our own destinies, believing that eating the apple allows us to become like God. O'Connor consistently challenges modern philosophy by denying its assumption of the self-sufficiency of humanity and forcing a realization of original sin that cannot be overcome by any human effort.

O'Connor understood that the result of seeing life in a modern, gnostic fashion is a divorce of feeling from its rightful source: Jesus Christ. Because modernity believes humans can solve their own problems, it denies the possibility of a mysterious solution that comes from outside of humanity, a solution that is God's. O'Connor wrote in a letter,

> The notion of the perfectibility of man came about at the time of the Enlightenment in the 18th century. . . . The Liberal approach is that man has never fallen, never incurred guilt, and is ultimately perfectible by his own efforts. Therefore, evil in this light is a problem of better housing, sanitation, health, etc. and all mysteries will eventually be cleared up. Judgment is out of place because man is not responsible.[59]

O'Connor's fiction is, in essence, a confrontation with the modern, liberal sensibility. She attempts to reintroduce judgment (which includes the possibility of grace) by establishing the reality of humanity's fall.

The South's defeat in the Civil War caused the South to have a heritage of loss and vulnerability that O'Connor found helpful in her task of revealing the fall. Her Southern characters instinctively reject modernity's self-righteousness, for Sherman's march incinerated their limitless progress.[60] O'Connor attacks "the Liberal approach" by allowing Southerners to incarnate the opposite of a liberal understanding of reality. She brings to "good country people" judgment that deems them swine and rains upon the criminal and insane sacramental grace that releases them from the lies of modernity and opens the door for their salvation.

Though the words of the old lady in Davison's seem harmlessly wrapped in the gentility of concern, they are in fact a veil for the greatest of all lies: that humans are independent and not dependent beings. Once unwrapped, the old lady's sentimentality indeed proves demonic. She is the serpent in the garden offering knowledge and reason as the solution to the problem of being a created being.

Faith Born from Suffering

The preceding has paid attention to how O'Connor's disability limited her as well as to O'Connor's positive view of limitation. Additionally, connections have been made between limitation and O'Connor's concern with debunking the myths of modernity. In order to develop further the theological significance of O'Connor's view of limitation, let us return to "Introduction to *A Memoir of Mary Ann,*" where O'Connor carefully develops her theological argument for an antidote to modernisms.

In the introduction, O'Connor writes about our cultural sentimentality and pity for those who suffer: "In this popular pity, we mark our gain in sensibility and our loss in vision. If other ages felt less, they saw more, even though they saw with the blind, prophetical, unsentimental eye of acceptance, which is to say, faith."[61] In contrast to modern culture, where suffering is rejected with absoluteness, "other ages" or premodern society accepted suffering as a given, and such acceptance was an act of faith. O'Connor continues, "In the absence of this faith now, we govern by tenderness. It is a tenderness which, long since cut off from the person of Christ, is wrapped in theory. When tenderness is detached from the source of tenderness, its logical outcome is terror. It ends in forced labor camps in the fumes of the gas chambers."[62]

As the Enlightenment began to explain the mysteries of moving stars, hurting spleens, and human development, it divorced the meaning of suffering from the revelation of Christ and his death. Once separated from the historical reality of God's suffering in Christ, suffering could no longer hold any meaning on its own and could only be viewed as evil.[63] The only option remaining for modernity was to use all the mechanisms of industrialization and science to force its own perception of good. To put it differently, when God is dead we are left to our own means for creating utopias.[64] O'Connor, like a prophet of old, judged that the devising of our own schemes ends in forced labor camps and eventually in the fumes of the gas chambers.

The jump from sentimentality, or tenderness, to the gas chamber is certainly a rather large leap, but her argument is strong. In congruence with a major concern the disability movement has over the eugenics of prenatal testing, O'Connor noted that the world influenced by modernism, which is "everywhere, . . . would not ask why Mary Ann should die, but why she should be born in the first place."[65] As will be shown later in discussing her stories, O'Connor made this point about eugenics multiple times. She perceived our society's trajectory toward prenatal testing and the resultant abortion of lives *presumably* filled with suffering.[66]

In order to avoid the presupposed suffering a Mary Ann or a Down syndrome child would incur, as well as the disruption of the pursuit of happiness for the parents, prenatal testing is now offered, and society regularly makes the choice that the disabled should not exist. O'Connor, of course, wrote her comments about Mary Ann well before *Roe v. Wade*, but she understood the cultural philosophies that are willing to, and feel they must, take not only death but also the possibility of life into their own hands in order to avoid suffering—*philosophies that begin with the simplicity of a sentimentality that desires to avoid suffering.* The connection between pity and actively killing people now becomes clear. O'Connor was, after all, not far removed from the utopian vision of the Third Reich that began its Holocaust with the disabled.

O'Connor wrote in a letter to Betty Hester, "There are times when the sharpest suffering is not to suffer and the worst affliction is not to be afflicted. Job's comforters were worse off than he was though they didn't know it."[67] True, Job's comforters did not seem worse off. They had not lost their children because of a west wind blowing a house down where their sons and daughters were gathered for a party. Their wives had not told them to curse God and die. But they were worse off because they did not understand the larger issues. Their lack of suffering allowed them to believe that justice and mercy were easily discernible, that consequences followed deeds simplistically. Their spiritual danger, then, was much greater than Job's. The logic Job's friends employ, often full of tenderness and pity, is clear in suggesting that an evil man should die, and so Job's nearness to death obviously proved his behavior had been evil.

In the first speech from one of Job's friends, Eliphaz makes the same movement O'Connor suggests, from tenderness to terror. Eliphaz begins by praising Job, saying that he has been a good man and encouraging him that his piety should be his comfort (Job 4:4-6). He quickly moves, though, through the logic of consequences following deeds to a dream/vision in which he understands that mortals are crushed more readily than a moth, are broken to pieces and unnoticed (4:19-20). Eliphaz then asks, "Call if you will, but who will answer you?" and directly links Job's suffering to God's justice. When one is caught up in a false philosophical system, be it modernism of our time or deeds-consequence of Job's time, one all too easily makes the jump from sentimentality for those who are suffering to believing that the killing of some people is right or righteous.

Job's next friend to speak picks up Eliphaz' stream of thought and begins by asking Job, "How long will you say such things? Your words are a blustering wind" (8:2). Bildad then tells Job, "When your children sinned against [God], he gave them over to the penalty of their sin" (8:4). The literary connection

between Job's words and sins and the wind that killed his children cannot be missed. All of Job's friends consider his crisis to
be part of God's justice. God, however, does not condone their
philosophy. God condemns them. Rather than offering a reason
for Job's suffering, God pushes Job into mystery. For O'Connor,
Job's suffering that leads to deeper mystery is better than the
misguided perspective of Job's friends that attempts to force an
ungodly justice onto the world even at the cost of killing people.

In the Mary Ann introduction, O'Connor continues her
defense against modernity, a defense that often turns lethal in
her stories. Looking at the picture of Mary Ann the sisters had
sent along with their original request for O'Connor to write
her story, O'Connor notes, "The child's picture had brought to
mind [Nathaniel Hawthorne's] story, 'The Birthmark.' "[68] Hawthorne's story concerns a prototypical modern scientist, Alymer,
and a small birthmark on his beautiful wife's face. His wife,
Georgiana, views her birthmark as a sign of beauty, but Alymer
explains to her, "you came so nearly perfect from the hand of
Nature that this slightest defect, which we hesitate to term a
defect or beauty, shocks me, as being the visible mark of earthly
imperfection."[69] Alymer then works to convince her that he
can safely rid her of this offense. Shortly after Alymer's science
removes the birthmark, which is perceived as a random act of
the "hand of Nature" instead of a part of the gift of life from
God, Georgiana dies.

In O'Connor's reading of the story, Georgiana's death is a
direct result of Alymer's confidence in the supremacy of the
scientific method, particularly its ability, even necessity, to overcome imperfection.[70] In "Introduction to *A Memoir of Mary
Ann*," O'Connor uses "The Birthmark" to call into question
the cultural philosophy of a society that attempts to eliminate
imperfections and suffering. The story also serves as a negative
analogy to the care Mary Ann received at the Our Lady of Perpetual Help Free Cancer Home. In contrast to the utopian science that kills Alymer's wife, Mary Ann was embraced "as is."
More important than her being protected from social stigma,

though, O'Connor says, was the fact that Mary Ann and the sisters "fashioned from her unfinished face the material of her death." Such a preparation for death is the "creative action of the Christian's life. . . . It is a continuous action in which this world's goods are utilized to the fullest, both positive gifts and what Pere Teilhard de Chardin calls 'passive diminishments.' Mary Ann's diminishment was extreme,"[71] but her particular Catholic education (not primarily a rational one) allowed her not only to endure such diminishment but to prepare her death in Christ, the most significant action of the Christian life.

O'Connor's theological embrace of disability is a far different understanding than the one persons with disabilities generally receive from the church: to endure until heaven. Suffering, in O'Connor's understanding, is not something to be avoided at all costs, something to hope to bypass. Rather, it is an inevitable part of life, a life that is fully a gift from the giver of life. To accept suffering is an act of faith that witnesses to the reality of this givenness. Only through the acceptance of suffering is it possible for God to be the alleviator of suffering. Only through the acceptance of suffering is it possible for the cross to have meaning. The acceptance of suffering is what made the cross possible for Christ. To accept what we perceive as good to be from God is a simple matter. To be able to look into the face of Mary Ann and see a face "full of promise," a face that is fully given and not half-taken or half-full of promise, is entirely different. O'Connor came to see her own suffering as something to be accepted, as part of what fills life with promise.[72] The mentions of acceptance in her letters, then, are not simplistic. She had developed a rich theology of acceptance, and she communicates her vision in her stories.

One further illustration will drive this point home. In O'Connor's theology, the size or amount of sufferings was not what created participation in Christ's sufferings. In one letter O'Connor addressed Betty Hester's concern about being stuck with people who do not love or understand her. The dark irony of this complaint in light of O'Connor's struggle with lupus and her death within the next year should not be lost as O'Connor's response is considered: "It all comes under the larger heading of what individuals have to suffer for the common good, a mystery, and part of the suffering of Christ."[73] To suggest that something as mundane as being stuck with people that do not understand you is a participation in Christ's suffering is nearly as counter-intuitive as the suggestion that sentimentality leads to the gas chambers. O'Connor, though, does not mean the "common good" as it would be defined and quantified philosophically as the greatest good for the greatest number of people, a definition that assumes the good is a matter of less pain and more pleasure. Rather, O'Connor means the authentic good that is God's and is thus commonly given to all humanity, and God's good often includes suffering. In "Introduction to *A Memoir of Mary Ann*," O'Connor writes concerning Alymer and modernists like him, "Busy cutting down human imperfection, they are making head-way also on the raw material of good."[74] The good is not found by the elimination of imperfection and suffering, for such in fact constitutes the raw material of the true good. Without suffering, the authentic good cannot be fashioned. What is good or bad for Hester, then, does not consist of external circumstances but is instead an interior fashioning that occurs in relation to external circumstances.

For O'Connor, a good based upon capability or eliminating suffering is necessarily inauthentic. O'Connor suggests a variant anthropology that embraces inability, particularly humanity's inability to save itself, over and against the modern presumption of self-sufficiency. Modernity's primary problem is the divorce of human need from the activity of God. Humanity has fancied itself sufficient unto itself. The placing of human capability at the center of meaning-making results in an inability to recognize, much less appreciate, the mysterious and necessary role dependence plays in human formation, not least of which is dependence on God. Furthermore, a culture that deems itself able to save itself from suffering is a culture that will necessarily marginalize and even demonize those who suffer, or those it believes are suffering, and will ultimately find ways to eliminate them, be it through positive developments in science or through gas chambers and prenatal testing.

Conclusion

Those who appreciate O'Connor have looked into the face of the grotesque in her work and recognized their own grinning, grotesque faces staring back at them. O'Connor's ability to break through our Enlightened visioning of the world and help us recognize our brokenness and sin is a great feat and may well be the most important aspect of her work. However, readers are drawn back to her work again and again because of a mystery that she leaves unexplained, a mystery that is unexplainable, a mystery that her fiction expands inside us. O'Connor wants us to look into the face of the grotesque and recognize Christ on the cross as the ultimate good. The connection between O'Connor's realization of this truth in her work and her involvement in telling the story of a disabled little girl who died young is no mere coincidence. O'Connor practiced living this mystery as she watched her father die and then dealt with the grotesqueries of the same disease herself. The mystery of the grotesque was more than a philosophical vantage point for her, more than a new paradigm of understanding. The mystery became real as it was mannered, just as God could not simply give new instructions but had to be enfleshed and had to suffer. The mystery is Christ's mystery. It is unwritable, yet its possibility can be felt in the afterglow of O'Connor's stories. As the nuns and O'Connor viewed her fiction through the lens of the cancer home that day, it was this unwritable mystery that merged their vocations into one revealing the deep, mannered truth they shared. The purpose of this book is to attempt to gain that same perspective by viewing O'Connor's fiction, and then the broader world, through the lens of her disability and limitations.

CHAPTER 2

The Grotesque Good
in O'Connor's Fiction

*The "mud in man" is nothing to be ashamed of. It can produce
. . . the face of God. . . . To recall this, to recall this incredible
relation between mud and God, is, in its own distant, adumbrat-
ing way, the function of comedy.*

—William Lynch, *Christ and Apollo*

There can be little doubt that the primary purpose of the
grotesque in O'Connor's fiction is to hold up a mirror to
her readers' own sin and weakness, to break through cultural
facades of strength and lay bare the human soul's deformities.
O'Connor provides a visible metaphor for a non-visible deficit and uses disability with great precision to accomplish her
task. Her grotesque characters challenge readers' perceptions
of "good" and "bad," exposing the perceived good—whether it
be sympathy, human progress, or "good" country people—as
actually well-endowed with original sin. Where disability is perceived negatively, it can remind us that we are all limited and all
carry a death sentence. For O'Connor, the implication concerns
more than a physical reality. Important to her is the truth that
we also all share a spiritual death sentence.

Many, if not most, of O'Connor's stories deal with social expectations of normality/abnormality and goodness/evil, ending with the reversal of these expectations. O'Connor's satirical deconstruction of the socially defined normal and good is also an ironic appreciation of difference and bad. The good she questions in "A Good Man Is Hard to Find," "A Stroke of Good Fortune," and "Good Country People" is society's misrepresentation of what is good. Opposed to this perceived good, the authentic good in her stories shows up in what are perceived as grotesque places. She reverses these social expectations perhaps most explicitly in the story "Revelation."

"Revelation"

From the very first paragraph of "Revelation," Mrs. Turpin sizes up and judges the occupants of the doctor's waiting room, beginning with their footwear. The white trash lady's shoes are "exactly what you would have expected her to have on."[1] Mrs. Turpin's social hierarchies, based upon physical appearance, provide the framework for the entire story. Later, referencing the "colored farm help," the narrator makes one of the most ironically misguided statements in O'Connor's work: "There was nothing you could tell [Mrs. Turpin] about people like them that she didn't know already."[2]

Mrs. Turpin's social constructs go far beyond simplistic social expectations of people and include the bigotry of naming the classes of people.

> On the bottom of the heap were most colored people, not the kind she would have been if she had been one, but most of them; then next to them—not above, just away from—were the white-trash; then above them were the home-owners, to which she and Claud belonged. Above she and Claud were people with a lot of money and much bigger houses and much more land. But here the complexity of it would begin to bear in on her.[3]

She gets confused because some people with good blood have lost their money and have to rent, while there is one colored man in town that owns two red Lincolns, a swimming pool, and a farm with registered white-faced cattle. "Usually by the time she had fallen asleep all the classes of people were moiling and roiling around in her head, and she would dream they were all crammed in together in a box car, being ridden off to be put in a gas oven."[4] The Holocaust image foreshadows the impending decimation of Mrs. Turpin's social constructs, but it also serves to remind the reader that all people share the same fate without deference to society's perception of them as good or bad, rich or poor.

At the beginning of the story, the waiting room where Mrs. Turpin and Claud have gone to get his leg examined is waiting for a revelation. The room itself is layered with grotesques. Mrs. Turpin is "very large," so much so that she is "a living demonstration that the room was inadequate and ridiculous."[5] Claud has an ulcer on his leg, "a purple swelling on a plump marble-white calf." The table is cluttered with "limp-looking magazines" and "a big green glass ash tray full of cigarette butts and cotton wads with little blood spots on them."[6]

The gravest grotesque in the room, though, is a silent college girl. Before Mary Grace's name is revealed halfway through the story, she is referenced as "ugly" nine times in as many pages. She is also called "a fat girl" and her skin is "blue with acne."[7] Her face is described as "seared" and "raw," and her eyes alternate between smoldering and blazing. Her actions and inactions are grotesque as well. She refuses to relinquish her seat in deference to social hierarchy, and she makes a face at Mrs. Turpin that is "the ugliest face Mrs. Turpin had ever seen anyone make."[8] O'Connor creates as much distance as possible between Mary Grace and Ruby Turpin's (and our) social conception of what is good. Yet this embodiment of everything we find ugly, annoying, and disrespectful becomes the vehicle for true grace in the story.

The reader is not given insight into Mary Grace's process of thinking; what causes her to heave the book at Mrs. Turpin is left unexplained. Perhaps Mary Grace has a psychological disorder or is demon-possessed. Or possibly she can no longer take the weight of social expectations that require her perfection. Or maybe she loathes her mother's hypocrisy and attacks a stranger in her place. Whatever the case, her deviation from social expectations becomes the gateway to reality for Mrs. Turpin. The grotesque thud of the book against Mrs. Turpin's forehead and the ensuing choking and condemnation that Mrs. Turpin is "a wart hog from hell" opens Mrs. Turpin to a mystery that contrasts profoundly with her seemingly well-grounded social hierarchies.

O'Connor finds the enormous distance created between Mary Grace's grotesqueries and Ruby Turpin's conception of the good to be just wide enough to hold a hint of the mystery of God's mercy. Mary Flannery felt the opening of such spaces, the invoking of such mystery, was a primary function of fiction. Her constant struggle as a writer was to make mystery real to those in the modern world whom she said were "a generation that has been made to feel that the aim of learning is to eliminate mystery."[9] Suffering and violence, she found, were particularly useful vehicles for conveying a "sense of mystery," a phrase she used repetitively in her essays.

Part of the usefulness of violence comes from its universality. We can all sympathize with the throbbing, intense pain that comes from a sudden, unexpected blow to the head. We all know what it is like to have someone we thought we were better than reveal to us our own limitations and hypocrisy. Unlike race or class, suffering remains distant to none. All experience pain and, like Job, ask, "Why me?" and upon further reflection about God, "Why anyone?" Fear of suffering and death pierces everyone and unearths our most profound questions about the meaning and purpose of life. Such piercing was all the more severe for O'Connor and the generation having just survived two world wars.

In lieu of his suffering, Job makes several chapters' worth of reasonable arguments to defend his innocence and question God's justice. Yet he receives no explanation. He is instead given a barrage of questions from God, a tutorial in mystery, and the question of why evil exists is ultimately left unanswered. Job's questions have not ceased at the end of the book—they have only changed, expanded, and deepened. O'Connor notes that fiction "leaves us like Job with a renewed sense of mystery,"[10] and she invokes Job's specific mystery in "Revelation." In the middle of the story, Mrs. Turpin is scowling at the ceiling, raising her fist, and making "a small stabbing motion over her chest as if she was defending her innocence to invisible guests who were like the comforters of Job, reasonable seeming but wrong."[11]

Job's "comforters" primarily told him suffering is a result of sin, a punishment from God. They had good and reasonable support for their arguments. God tells the Israelites time and again in the Pentateuch that if they will only keep the commandments, all will go well for them in the new land. However, if they disobey, disease and death will come to them, and the land will be taken away. Disease-as-punishment was common sense in Job's time, so his boils proved his sin. Like Job, though with much less cause for it, Mrs. Turpin also figures herself righteous. She stands amongst her pigs, wrestling with the revelation that she is a wart hog from hell. She wonders why she, a "good" person, is being punished and asks, "How am I a hog and me both?"[12] Her social categories justify her, yet as the story progresses the revelation that she is a hog continues to open her up from the inside, deconstructing her social hierarchy.

Job demands proof of his transgressions and questions God's motives. When God finally responds, he demands to know who Job thinks he is that he can presume to put the Almighty on trial. In the next-to-last scene of "Revelation," Ruby Turpin, still standing in the pig parlor, defends her work ethic and her charitableness to the church and even to the "trash around here," "black and white."[13] Her questioning climaxes in a desperate challenge:

> A final surge of fury shook her and she roared, "Who do you think you are?"
>   The color of everything, field and crimson sky, burned for a moment with a transparent intensity. The question carried over the pasture and across the highway and the cotton field and returned to her like an answer from beyond the wood.[14]

Frustrated and confused, she hurls her question out into creation, demanding that the Almighty answer for the unjust actions toward her. Creation echoes back to her the question she asked: "Who do you think you are?" Her inquiry into identity is the same question Job asked of God and the same question God asked Job and now asks Ruby. When God asks Job who he is (Job 38–39), Job is unable to respond (40:1-5). The following line in O'Connor's story again echoes Job's: "[Ruby] opened her mouth but no sound came out of it."[15] Mrs. Turpin's entry into mystery is what O'Connor finds essential, and often suffering is the means of awakening her characters to such mystery.

O'Connor's and Job's revelations from living with and struggling with suffering contrast sharply with the pastoral platitudes and expectations of Job's friends and current popular theologies. In O'Connor's and Job's revelations, there is no self-serving lesson to be gained, no better person for having endured the struggles God brought about, no good life now or purpose-driven existence. The suffering is not utilitarian. If it were, Job's and Mrs. Turpin's questioning would be justified, for surely God's goodness and power could bring about change without employing suffering. No justification for evil is given, though, and Job and Mrs. Turpin are instead opened to the mystery of being vulnerable humans, as surely O'Connor's own struggle with disability did for her. Suffering serves for O'Connor as a gateway to this mysterious reality of our universal limitedness and inability to save ourselves, a revelation that came more and more to the fore of O'Connor's fiction the closer she came to death, which is why it is portrayed so clearly in "Revelation," published the year of her death.

Ruby Turpin's encounter with suffering, both the physical suffering from early in the story and the mental anguish of falling from the top of her social hierarchy in the remainder of the story, opens her to the mysterious revelation at the story's end, where she has a vision of a bridge "extending upward from the earth through a field of living fire." A horde of souls are rumbling toward heaven, and those closest to heaven on the bridge are the white trash, the coloreds, and "battalions of freaks and lunatics shouting and clapping and leaping like frogs." Such Pentecostal inappropriateness comes across to O'Connor's audience as a grotesque vision.

> And bringing up the end of the procession was a tribe of people whom she recognized at once as those who, like herself and Claud, had always had a little of everything and the God-given wit to use it right. They were marching behind the others with great dignity, accountable as they had always been for good order and common sense and respectable behavior. They alone were on key. Yet she could see by their shocked and altered faces that even their virtues were being burned away.[16]

All that she has known as a "good," God-lovin' country person has not put her in the front of the line. Instead, the first are last, and the shouting and clapping freaks and lunatics have leapt to the front. O'Connor's deconstruction of Mrs. Turpin's categorizations of the perceived good is simultaneously an appreciation of the authentic good found in the freaks and lunatics who shall enter first. In other words, "Revelation" fully reverses the social expectations Mrs. Turpin had at the beginning of the story, not only humbling the haughty but also elevating the humble. And the key to Mrs. Turpin's corrected vision of the world is the suffering she experiences, a suffering that is common to us all.

"The Lame Shall Enter First"

These freaks entering heaven first causes one to remember O'Connor's encounter with the old lady at Davison's, in which she imagines the lame using their crutches to get to the front of heaven's line. In relating the elevator story, O'Connor rejected the way society conflates a person's limitation with his or her identity. In the year following that shopping trip to Davison's, O'Connor crafted "The Lame Shall Enter First," which uses disability and fascination with ailment to expose modernity's tendency to obsess over fixing visible problems while ignoring spiritual crises.

In "The Lame Shall Enter First," a social worker named Sheppard takes in a delinquent child named Rufus Johnson and showers him with attention while ignoring his own son, whom he views as selfish and dumb. Sheppard works at a reformatory, and when he meets Rufus at their first interview, he sees that "a kind of fanatic intelligence was palpable in his face." He also sees the boy has "a monstrous club foot," and he quickly infers the boy's problem: "The case was clear to Sheppard instantly. His mischief was compensation for the foot."[17] As the story progresses, Sheppard infuses the foot with greater and greater meaning and totalizes the boy according to his foot. Since he believes the foot is the source of all the boy's problems and the boy is just one big problem, for Sheppard the foot is the boy and the boy is the foot, and until the foot gets fixed the boy will remain monstrous as well, both visibly and ethically.

Sheppard's interaction with Rufus is well intentioned. The reformer takes the troublemaker into his home, feeds him, clothes him, and spares no expense to acquire the specially fitted shoe that will help Rufus walk without a limp. Yet all of Sheppard's progressiveness proves to be no more than the sentimentality O'Connor so profoundly rejected. Sheppard's sentimentality eventually crumbles beneath the weight of reality, and Sheppard begins to feel toward the boy the repulsion he feels toward the foot:

> The boy's clubfoot was set within the circle of his vision. The pieced-together shoe appeared to grin at him with Johnson's own face. He caught hold of the edge of the sofa cushion and his knuckles turned white. A chill of hatred shook him. He hated the shoe, hated the foot, hated the boy. His face paled. Hatred choked him. He was aghast at himself.[18]

Following the modern, Enlightened sensibility, Sheppard believes that if he can fix the shoe the boy will cease being delinquent and will be able to reenter society as a normal child. Sheppard's sentimentality toward the boy was never a true acceptance of his life, though; his sentimentality was only an acceptance of the ideal life Sheppard imagined for the boy. As his ability to fix Rufus fails, so too does his sentimentality toward the boy, and he finds he hates that which he cannot fix.

At the story's end, Sheppard tells Rufus, "You're not evil, you're mortally confused. You don't have to make up for that foot, you don't have to. . . ." But Rufus knows Sheppard cannot fix him. He hurls "himself forward. 'Listen at him!' he scream[s]. 'I lie and steal because I'm good at it! My foot don't have a thing to do with it! The lame shall enter first! The halt'll be gathered together. When I get ready to be saved, Jesus'll save me, not that lying stinking atheist, not that . . .' "[19] Rufus refuses to be defined by his limitation, to be totalized according to it. The foot is not the sum of his being. He will not allow his foot to take the blame for his sin, and he understands that if he did, there would be no need for Jesus. And so O'Connor stepped off the elevator at Davison's.

Running parallel to the theme of Sheppard totalizing the boy and trying to fix the clubbed foot is O'Connor's unveiling of the sin within the major characters. When Rufus removes his shoe, "The unsheathed mass of foot in the dirty sock made Sheppard feel queasy. He turned his eyes away until the new shoe was on." Sheppard's modernized vision causes physical repulsion when he is confronted with deformity. O'Connor then uses similar language to describe the shoe and Sheppard's interior. The new shoe is "a black slick shapeless object, shining hideously."[20] As Sheppard wearies of his unsuccessful struggles to fix the boy, the reader gets a glimpse of Sheppard's parallel interior. He gets angry with Rufus and looks into his eyes, which "were like distorting mirrors in which he saw himself made hideous and grotesque."[21] As O'Connor does in many of her stories, the outer grotesqueries of her characters parallel, and stand as metaphor for, the inner grotesqueries of her characters and her readers. In this story, though, the disability is not a representation of Rufus' moral lack, as is the case with Joy/Hulga in "Good Country People," but instead represents Sheppard's, and society's, misunderstanding of the disabled person and of the shared human condition of vulnerability.[22]

The end of the story reveals O'Connor's philosophical/ theological concern. Sheppard's overly ambitious sentimentality toward Rufus causes complete disregard for his own son, who desperately needs his father's help in dealing with his mother's recent death. Since the modern perspective can only diagnose and understand the physical, Sheppard is unable to relate to his son's grief and confusion. For Sheppard, his wife has simply ceased to be, and he must move on.

In the story's closing scene, Sheppard finds his son, who has committed suicide in the attic—"hung in the jungle of shadows, just below the beam from which he had launched his flight into space."[23] Sheppard has missed his son's spiritual crisis and in so doing has killed his child. O'Connor's intention here is clear: modernity is on trial, for it has fashioned this child's gallows.

But O'Connor does not offer an answer to the modern crisis. Instead, she draws the landscape so profoundly that when we ask her characters who they think they are, the question echoes back across the large, mysterious spaces and assaults us. O'Connor filled the role of a John the Baptist, announcing judgment and calling people to accept the fact of their sin. Her particular calling was to prepare the way, and in "The Lame Shall Enter First," acceptance of deformity, both of Rufus' physical foot and the son's spiritual confusion, is the necessary first step.

"Revelation" and "The Lame Shall Enter First" are two very different stories, but they are both about people who are unable to accept limitations, to accept our common human fallenness. Mrs. Turpin cannot accept her own limitation, and Sheppard cannot accept anyone else's. Though one is a Christian and the other is decidedly not so, their denial of the fall is one and the same, and it takes extreme suffering for either of them to catch a glimpse of the mysterious truth that is common vulnerable humanity. In the story about the Christian, we are given a glimpse of a new possibility, a different social hierarchy in which the first shall be last. In the story about the penultimate modernist, we are left only with the unsolvable mystery of death.

The Role of Acceptance

Recognizing O'Connor's emphasis on sin in her stories is not difficult and has been well expounded.[24] Original sin is the indictment with which the grandmother comes to terms and the Misfit cannot accept in "A Good Man Is Hard to Find." It is the wooden part of Joy/Hulga's soul in "Good Country People." Original sin cuts through all the social constructions of the good in "The Displaced Person" to allow/cause the death of the DP.

Having identified modernity's great sin, O'Connor's answer is profound in its simplicity: acceptance. Only when her characters can accept themselves as limited, vulnerable, and sinful does there arise even the possibility for grace.[25] Until people accept the reality of limitation and vulnerability, they will continue to feel they can fix their problems and thus have no need of a savior. Without the acceptance of sin and limitation as unsurprising aspects of being human, there is no desire to go down into the water of baptism and die to self, and there is no possibility of being raised up to new life. Like John the Baptist in the wilderness eating locusts and honey, O'Connor stood in all her splendid oddity calling the whole of modernity to realize its own ineptitude and to repent and be baptized. O'Connor's acceptance of limitation is the beginning point and essence of her work, a prophetic cry she makes most explicit in the stories "A Temple of the Holy Ghost" and "The Enduring Chill."

Though already noted, the point cannot be overstated that the basic problem O'Connor has with modernity is its belief in the perfectibility of humanity by its own efforts. Modernity consequently misconceives the authentic good. In contrast to the modern attempt to define and create its own good, O'Connor believes the authentic good must be received, and accepting it begins with accepting the need for a good that is outside the self and even outside of humanity's efforts altogether. O'Connor's first step of acknowledging our shared *inabilities* stands in sharp contrast to the Enlightened idea that the first step in the process of becoming better humans is an acknowledgment of every person's equal *ability* to accomplish.

In "A Temple of the Holy Ghost" and "The Enduring Chill," O'Connor again uses the grotesque as metaphor. Nevertheless, she meant for her grotesques always to function also within reality, even in her early stories such as "Good Country People."

Certainly Joy/Hulga's wooden leg works on a metaphorical level
to represent the corresponding "wooden part of her soul," but
O'Connor insists on more. She writes, "If you want to say that
the wooden leg is a symbol, you can say that. But it is a wooden
leg first, and as a wooden leg it is absolutely necessary to the
story. It has its place on the literal level of the story, but it operates in depth as well as on the surface."[26] O'Connor's insistence
upon and attention to the literal level is what helps her uses
of limitation not be mere representations of evil. They are real
for her characters and her stories. Thus, her use of disability, for
example, does not pull the reader away from the story in order to
make a philosophical point. Rather, the disability works within
the story and remains true to the reality of the character with
the disability. O'Connor's skill in using disability in this way is
surely a result of her own familiarity with disability, but also has
very important philosophical and theological underpinnings.

Whether or not her symbolic limitations also work on the
literal level is essential to O'Connor's purpose. In writing her
style of fiction, a style attempting to open the reader to mystery,
she worked hard to resist the constant danger of reducing her
fiction to mere metaphors for spirituality. As she expressed to
her friend Betty Hester, her primary question in writing was, "Is
it believable?" In O'Connor's understanding, presenting fiction
only as merely symbolic backfires because the artist becomes
Manichean, placing the spiritual at odds with the physical.[27] The
way to avoid Manichaeism is to make the fiction not just generally real to ultimate truths, but particularly real to the details
of life's experience. Indeed, the possibility for mystery is created only in the tension that occurs in the joining of the general
with the particular. Continuing her letter to Hester, she writes,
"I don't believe that in all this [writing] you can be so cavalier
about particulars. When the particulars are wrong, the general
is usually wrong too. If you are too cavalier about the particulars you will find yourself a Manichean without knowing how it
happened."[28]

Part of her understanding of the meaning of Manichaeism comes from her reading of the scholarly Jesuit William F. Lynch. George Kilcourse has explored O'Connor's work in light of Lynch's distinction between the Manichean and the christological imaginations—the Manichean imagination's separation of matter from spirit and the christological imagination's "patient movement through the 'human mysteries.'"[29] Kilcourse writes,

> As Lynch outlines in the second installment of his essay, "Theology and Imagination," there is a Manichaean temptation for the imagination "to win its freedom by seeking quick infinities through the rapid and clever manipulation of the finite" instead of passing through "all the rigors, densities, limitations, and decisions of the actual." Here are the makings of an ascetic identity that O'Connor will employ in creating her characters.[30]

To avoid a Manichean split between spirit and matter in her writing, O'Connor focused on making people's manners true to the density of experience. The result, or perhaps the fountain, is richly incarnational theology.[31] The general truths come to us *only* through the particularities and limitations of the everyday. In other words, she believed mystery comes through manners— or even more succinctly, she believed deeply in the incarnation.

Writing about "A Good Man Is Hard to Find," O'Connor noted that "what makes a story work, and what makes it hold up as a story" often comes down to a single gesture in the story: "This would have to be an action or a gesture which was both totally right and totally unexpected; it would have to be one that was both in character and beyond character; it would have to suggest both the world and eternity."[32] Whether or not she succeeds in making her characters' gestures both true to reality and open to mystery cannot be critiqued, only witnessed. Whether or not she succeeds, one thing is certain: for O'Connor mystery is wedded to manners, and if the manners are not true to reality, the mystery cannot be realized. And in her understanding, in order for manners to be true to reality, the writer (and reader) must accept "all the rigors, densities, *limitations*, and decisions of the actual."[33] Encounters with mystery, the purpose of O'Connor's fiction, can only occur in relation to the limitation of being. On a most basic level, then, O'Connor's fiction depends upon an acceptance of limitation.

Acceptance is also key spiritually, for O'Connor believed one's limitations and creatureliness must be accepted before redemption can become a possibility. Only a few months before her death, she wrote in a letter, "The writer has to make corruption believable before he can make the grace meaningful,"[34] and she purposed to make her grotesquely drawn characters real in a way that allowed her readers to see themselves in the characters. Any skipping over the densities of reality would forfeit the possibility of opening her readers to mystery.

O'Connor wrote in "The Fiction Writer and His Country" that "to know oneself is, above all, to know what one lacks. It is to measure oneself against Truth, and not the other way around. The first product of self-knowledge is humility."[35] The first product is humility for O'Connor because true self-knowledge must begin with acceptance of original sin—that we are all born limited and corrupt. O'Connor not only understood her own stories as being "stories about original sin," but she understood all drama in the same terms. She wrote in "Novelist and Believer," "The serious writer has always taken the flaw in human nature for his starting point, usually the flaw in an otherwise admirable character. Drama usually bases itself on the bedrock of original sin, whether the writer thinks in theological terms or not."[36]

Because of original sin's primacy and modernity's inability to perceive it, O'Connor's own brand of particularity most often portrays the generality of original sin. Making original sin believable is the most consistent theme in her fiction. She helps readers perceive the reality of limitations and accept vulnerability, which then allows possible openness to the mysterious ways of God's work in the world. Acceptance, however, is primary. Before revelation can come, before God can act, before evil can be transformed, the need must be realized. Again, for the Enlightenment-influenced, recognizing need means looking beyond being taught that the world is conquerable and instead *accepting* vulnerabilities, abnormalities, and our inability to save ourselves from everything. If Sheppard could have accepted his own son's limitations, he would have saved the boy, and the same may well be true for Rufus.

Acceptance in "A Temple of the Holy Ghost"

Though most of O'Connor's portrayals of acceptance happen as negative examples, as with "The Enduring Chill," there are at least a couple of positive portrayals of acceptance, as was seen in "Revelation" but is perhaps best done in "A Temple of the Holy Ghost." The story contrasts the town's lack of acceptance of the hermaphrodite with the hermaphrodite's full acceptance of his/her own life. Society totalizes the hermaphrodite according to his/her abnormality, and he/she is able to survive economically only as part of a freak show at town fairs. When the fair comes to the setting of "A Temple of the Holy Ghost," the local preachers and police so fear the hermaphrodite's inability to be categorized that they shut down the fair and run the hermaphrodite and the entire fair out of town.

The story's protagonist, an unnamed twelve-year-old girl, is told about the hermaphrodite by her cousins, who saw the hermaphrodite the day before the tents came down. They relate the hermaphrodite's stage act, and how he/she spoke to the people, saying, "God made me thisaway and if you laugh He may strike you the same way. This is the way He wanted me to be and I ain't disputing His way." The hermaphrodite accepts his/her lot and is in his/her own words "making the best of it."[37] He/she also points out the universal possibility for disability to "strike" anyone.

Upon hearing the story, the main character goes to bed trying to figure out how the hermaphrodite could be both male and female without having two heads. She sleepily imagines the scene and lapses into a dream. In her dream/vision, she reimagines the stage act as a church revival, and the hermaphrodite's acceptance of his/her condition comes even more to the fore. The hermaphrodite repeats that "God made me thisaway and I don't dispute hit," and the people reply with amens. He/she then exclaims, "God done this to me and I praise Him." Amens again follow. He/she tells the people they are temples of the

Holy Ghost and God's Spirit has a dwelling in them, which they of course agree with, repeating their amens. Finally, he/she warns them not to desecrate the temple and reminds them that if they laugh God may strike them "thisaway." He/she ends by claiming, "I am a temple of the Holy Ghost," to which they all agree with a final "Amen."[38]

The next morning the girl attends Benediction, having accepted, at least in her subconsciousness, that the hermaphrodite is a temple of the Holy Ghost. Perhaps resulting from her newfound acceptance, the girl realizes for the first time that she is in the presence of God and has a change of heart about the rudeness she has portrayed throughout the story, especially toward her mother. Her acceptance of life as given has led directly to the need to accept her own sin. She asks God to help her stop sassing. O'Connor may have chosen the Benediction service because of a line from one of its hymns: "Faith for all defects supplying, Where the feeble senses fail." In case her readers have missed the connection, O'Connor lays it out rather vividly. As Benediction begins, the freak-show dream recaptures the girl's thoughts and becomes incorporated into the most significant of sacraments. "Her mind began to get quiet and then empty but when the priest raised the monstrance with the Host shining ivory-colored in the center of it, she was thinking of the tent at the fair that had the freak in it. The freak was saying 'I don't dispute hit. This is the way He wanted me to be.' "[39] In this scene, O'Connor equates the hermaphrodite's acceptance of life-as-is with Christ's acceptance of the call to be the sacrificial Lamb of God. The monstrous and the Monstrance become one in the girl's imagination, a result of her dream encounter with the hermaphrodite. The hermaphrodite's acceptance of his/her condition is bound together with the girl's acceptance of her mother, herself, and the raised "Monstrance" with the Host, as well as with Christ's acceptance of being human and broken.

The story ends with the girl riding home from Benediction, looking out the window. She is "lost in thought." O'Connor's last line paints the meaning of the Eucharist upon the landscape, leaving the reader with the mental image of a blood-soaked Christ hanging on a tree. This scene shows how the girl's experience has changed not only the child's desire to be sassy, but her view of the world. "The sun was a huge red ball like an elevated Host drenched in blood and when it sank out of sight, it left a line in the sky like a red clay road hanging over the trees."[40] The physical "deformity" and social exclusion of the hermaphrodite have helped the girl understand the meaning of Christ's passion. She is thus opened to the deeper mysteries of life because the hermaphrodite's acceptance of his/her condition has become her gateway to reality.[41]

The child's realization is set in sharp contrast to the girl's cousins, whose concern for their bodies being temples trumps any concern for the Holy Ghost's movement.[42] Buying into the cultural construct that their young bodies make them "perfect," these girls are unable to accept their state as fallen creatures or to recognize any need for redemption and salvation. They are unable to understand how they are temples of the Holy Ghost, and instead view their temple status as a mere joke, mockingly naming themselves temple one and temple two.

O'Connor's reviewers have not always understood what she was attempting to get across in her stories. Her response to one such critical misunderstanding was to remark, "When I see these stories described as horror stories I am always amused because the reviewer always has hold of the wrong horror."[43] The real horrors in "A Temple of the Holy Ghost" are the lack of acceptance offered by the community to the hermaphrodite and the judgmental attitudes of the cousins. The horror is not the hermaphrodite. Indeed, the hermaphrodite is the story's one pure character, which is again an example of how O'Connor turns social expectations upside down and portrays grace in what society deems grotesque.

O'Connor later wrote in a letter that what the girl in the story learns is purity, which is surely an odd thing to learn from a hermaphrodite in a freak show, at least until one understands what O'Connor means by purity. She goes on in the letter to define purity as "an acceptance of what God wills for us, an acceptance of our individual circumstances."[44] O'Connor's definition sounds like a pastoral platitude meant to encourage one who has recently experienced a tragedy. Parents who give birth to disabled children are told that it is all part of God's greater purpose, and if they can just accept that, God will be their strength. People who are diagnosed with cancer are told God has a reason for allowing their disease. What is different in O'Connor's belief about the significance of acceptance, though, is that she is not sentimentally encouraging those overwhelmed by a tragedy. Rather, she is defining purity.

Society thinks of purity as innocence and/or an absence of defects: purity is the ideal form, and the greater the defects one has, the further one moves away from purity. A cancerous body is less pure than one without cancer. One problem with society's definition is that the ideal is always culturally defined. For cultures that are children of the Enlightenment, the ideal or pure form means autonomy and efficiency. Any antonym of these, such as vulnerability, smacks of impurity and evil. Innocence and vulnerability, however, have nothing to do with purity, nor can purity be measured in relation to any physical standards of perfection. O'Connor's definition of purity as the hermaphrodite's acceptance of the given circumstances of his/her life makes purity an attitude of the heart toward life, an attitude that accepts life as given, including all its densities and limitations. For O'Connor, the *circumstance* of the given is not where good or evil resides. Rather, good and evil reside in a person's *response* to the circumstance. All formulas for what makes a person "normal" or pure either physically or mentally are deconstructed by O'Connor's definition. Instead, the pure heart O'Connor defines begins to find God at work in circumstances that society views as grotesque, undesirable, inefficient, and/or disabled. O'Connor's stories are meant to purify her readers on this level.

Acceptance in "The Enduring Chill"

O'Connor portrays the devastating results of a lack of acceptance in "The Enduring Chill." The story's first page paints a picture that is transposed from O'Connor's own life. Because of an illness, Asbury has been forced to return home to live with his mother. He returns from New York on a train and finds his mother waiting for him in his rural hometown. Not only do these circumstances mirror O'Connor's own, Asbury's sickness is also very similar. Asbury "was puffy and pale and his hair had receded tragically for a boy of twenty-five."[45] O'Connor was twenty-five when she was diagnosed with lupus and returned to live with her mother, and her medications caused puffiness, hair loss, and intolerance to the sun. Asbury has also been experiencing "a gradual slackening of his energy and vague inconsistent aches and headaches," as was the case for O'Connor. Asbury is an artist, a calling neither his family nor O'Connor's embraced or fully understood. Inasmuch as their families accept their talents, they are both encouraged to write "good" Southern fiction, like another *Gone with the Wind*.[46]

Unlike O'Connor, though, Asbury does not learn purity: he does not accept his changed circumstances. Though resistant at first ("when I faced it I was roped and tied and resigned the way it is necessary to be resigned to death"), O'Connor's attitude toward her return to the South eventually displayed purity. She accepted the disease and its consequences for her. Asbury, on the other hand, so rejects his life change that he even refuses the help of the local physician Dr. Block, continuously claiming that what is wrong with him is way beyond Dr. Block. He also rejects the "collapsing country junction" that is his hometown, talk about the cattle, help opening his suitcase, breakfast, his mother's continuous advice, her good intentions and good wishes for him, his writing, and ultimately his "useless life."

The only thing he embraces is his illness, though not his true illness, only the imagined effect his death will have upon his mother. Before leaving New York, he wrote a letter to her that filled two notebooks, explaining her role in making his life a failure, and he relished the idea that "because of the letter, she might experience a painful realization and this would be the only thing of value he had to leave her."[47] However, despite accepting a false demise, having "become entirely accustomed to the thought of death," his frustration with having to return home left him unaccustomed "to the thought of death *here.*"[48] In New York, amongst his intellectual friends such as Goetz, death is meaningless and thereby acceptable. Here, however, the culture and his family so press meaning upon him that his death can only be useful if it teaches someone about life's meaninglessness. To this end, Asbury accepts the false illness unto death that will teach his mother a lesson, but not the actual illness that he has brought upon himself.

As Asbury's condition worsens, he demands as a dying request to see a Jesuit priest, for he once ran across one and found him well educated. He thinks if he can get such a priest to visit he can have some intellectual conversation to escape the talk about cows and their reproduction. When the priest finally arrives, he is not interested in Asbury's attempts at educated discourse. Instead, the priest primarily asks Asbury whether or not he says prayers. The only other question he asks before trying to start the catechism is, "Do you have trouble with purity?" His question seems, from the normal understanding of what purity is, a rather odd one to be included in the very few that the priest asks before he is kicked out. However, when considered in light of O'Connor's definition of purity-as-acceptance, the question is essential to Asbury's spiritual condition. The priest's question about purity is whether or not Asbury has accepted his circumstances, and the answer is the same as the one Asbury gives to the question of whether he knows his catechism: "Certainly not."

Disregarding Asbury's negative response, the priest begins the catechism anyway: "Who made you?" Asbury replies, "Different people believe different things about that." Asbury's most basic problem is one of purity because he has not accepted the conditions of his life, from his mother's identity to his exile in a rural town to the essential knowledge of being one who has been created. Without acceptance, he remains unprepared for grace.

The end of the story finds Asbury feeling "as if he were a shell that had to be filled with something but he did not know what."[49] O'Connor's description works both on the physical level, as his sickness worsens, and on a spiritual level. Convinced that death is approaching quickly, he realizes his god, Art, and his philosophies have left him empty, and he is tormented "thinking of his useless life."[50] Instructed by modernity that the good of life is measured by accomplishment, Asbury's lack of accomplishment has left him a mere shell of an Enlightened human being.

Of course, the last pages of the story reveal that Asbury is not dying at all, but only has undulant fever, which he obtained by drinking unpasteurized milk in an effort to bond with the "negroes" who worked on his mother's dairy farm. Only once he has been forced to *accept* the truth of his circumstances is he made *pure* enough for the change that is to come upon him. In the story's final scene, Asbury lies in bed feeling sicker than ever and looks into the mirror and finds that his eyes seem paler: "They looked shocked clean as if they had been prepared for some awful vision about to come down on him." Asbury turns his head and stares at the water stain of a fierce bird on his ceiling. The bird suddenly appears to be in motion, descending upon him like the Holy Ghost. The narrator notes, "The old life in him was exhausted. He awaited the coming of new." As the bird begins moving, "Asbury blanche[s] and the last film of illusion [is] torn as if by a whirlwind from his eyes."[51] The story then ends with the Holy Ghost's implacable descent upon the boy.

Asbury's illness acts negatively as his means of grace. The illness creates such weakness and vulnerability in him that he is forced to reckon with ultimate questions about who he is as a human being, questions about who created him and what purpose he has in life as well as his relation to those around him, especially his family. His lack of acceptance of anything in the story, even his own writings, reveals just how impure the boy is. However, the truth that his illness is only undulant fever unveils his self-righteous behavior toward the "negroes" and his family. Once his vision is thereby "shocked clean" and the "last film of illusion" has been torn from his eyes, he is prepared for the warm (and enduring) chill that the Holy Ghost's descent causes. Asbury's illness becomes his gateway to reality as it eventually leads him to realize his vulnerability.

O'Connor does not, however, portray the illness as salvific or evil. Nor does she use the illness as a tool to bring about God's purposes. Rather, the illness is the story's given, its atmosphere. Asbury's response to the illness, his movement from not accepting to accepting, begins his purification and readies him for the Holy Ghost's descent. The movement from denial to acceptance is what makes the story alive, both in its own action and in the reader's response to the story. Before the reality of the illness deconstructs him, Asbury accepts the illness on false pretense: "Asbury Fox was prone to the dramatic and was convinced that his suffering was the price to pay for his artistic inclinations, just as other great artists had suffered for their art."[52] He accepts his illness as a gift from his god, Art, and he perceives it as a trade-off for talent, which is what some have wrongly thought was O'Connor's perception of her illness. He also sentimentalizes his seemingly impending death as the one thing that can cause his mother to see his (and her) life clearly.[53]

For O'Connor, however, sentimentality is useless. Indeed, it must be fled, even if one is on crutches and the elevator has not arrived at the correct floor. Asbury's sentimentality is no more than a veil for a lack of acceptance of his illness' true reality and is therefore emblematic only of a lack of purity in his life more generally. The Holy Ghost can descend upon the temple that is Asbury only once he has been forced to accept his limitations. The priest's question of whether the boy struggles with purity is therefore telling for the boy and the reader, as is the priest's subsequent statement, "We all do but you must pray to the Holy Ghost for it."[54]

At an O'Connor conference held at Loyola University in 2011, Bill Sessions read from an unreleased diary O'Connor wrote while at the Iowa Writers' Workshop. O'Connor used the journal as a means of prayer. In the selection Sessions read,

O'Connor prayed over her struggle with her limitations as a writer. She most profoundly feared being mediocre. Nevertheless, and even at this young age, she grasped the significance of acceptance. She prayed earnestly that God not allow her to be mediocre, yet also wrote that mediocrity was "something I'll have to submit to if it is my scourge."

As we know, mediocrity did not become her scourge. Her willingness, though, to accept even this greatest of her fears, may well be what kept her from being mediocre. She also prayed about suffering, which she somehow knew was needed. "It is hard to want to suffer," she wrote. "I feel too mediocre to suffer. God have mercy on me." These most intimate yearnings and fears revealed in her prayer journal help us understand the disposition by which she was able to accept lupus and its consequences for her life and her early death. We can see clearly why her stories portray God's "mercy on me" in such powerfully and painfully real ways.

CHAPTER 3

Baptizing Modernity

Mary, the Mother of Jesus

Like Mary Grace, Mary the mother of Jesus was grotesque.
We are not accustomed to thinking of Mary as grotesque.
We think of her primarily at Christmas as the pure virgin servant found worthy enough to bear the Christ child. But what is
our vision of her purity—sexual, moral, beautiful, loving, all of
these? Asking this question problematizes our cultural definitions of the good. Can we, for example, envision Mary as disabled, with only one arm or one eye or with a mental disability
that caused her to see "visions"? Was she nearsighted? What illnesses did she suffer in her life? Certainly this unwed mother
did not fit into her culture's definition of perfection; pure was
likely one of the last descriptors the townspeople of Nazareth
would have used for her at the time. There is no historical evidence concerning her appearance, her health, or her mental
stability, yet somehow her "wholeness" seems significant to us.
We project our constructions of perfection upon her. As with
our images of Jesus, our representation of Mary has historically
been the ideal version of who we want to be, evidenced by the

idealized versions of Christ's birth that emerge yearly in count-
less nativity scenes.

The one qualification the biblical record does present for the
peasant girl Mary is her *willingness* to be the womb that knit God
and humanity into one person. Mary is, of course, afraid when
the angel comes to her, and she asks how she will bear a child
since she is a virgin. The angel's answer, "The Holy Spirit will
come upon you," is by no means clear. Mary must have still been
confused and afraid. Yet her response to the angel is, "I am the
Lord's servant. May your word to me be fulfilled."[1] The purity
the biblical record attests of Mary is not our usual definition of
purity but is instead O'Connor's definition of purity: accepting
the extraordinary circumstances given her.

In Mary's faithful act of being a womb, she became our greatest example of God's activity in the world. In her, we learn that
Immanuel, "God with us," is not conjured up by our readiness,
strength, or expertise. We also learn that God's kingdom does
not obliterate human limitation with limitless ability. Instead,
human limitation and God are woven together, and the presence of the Almighty in the world mysteriously involves divinity
taking limitation onto God's very being. A new perspective on
O'Connor's fiction works the same way.

At the opening of this chapter I asserted that Mary is grotesque in hopes of providing a focal point for O'Connor's deconstruction of our cultural definitions of what is grotesque and
explicating in its place O'Connor's theology of weakness (more
on a theology of weakness in the following chapter). In contrast
to our usual definitions of purity as the absence of flaw or limitation, which is also part of our definition of the good, O'Connor
makes the theological assertion that the tumored face of Mary
Ann and the mean, blue-acned face of Mary Grace are both
the face of Mary, Christ's mother, and the true face of us all in
our limited yet divinely infused humanity. Mary Ann and Mary,
Christ's mother, are one and the same, and it is not their purity-
as-innocence that distinguishes them but their purity-as-acceptance. Their limitations operate paradoxically both as results of

the fall and as loci for God's presence in the world. God chooses limited Marys as agents of revelation: not conceptual revelation, but the Almighty taking actual, physical limitation into God's self in order to be revealed to us.

Mary the mother of Christ, whom Wordsworth called "Our tainted nature's solitary boast,"[2] signifies God's work in us in that our common, human limitation is the womb for Immanuel, God with us—God's grace inside, connected with, grafted into a grotesque and limited humanity. Again, the temptation is to understand limitation as the womb for God as a mere paradigm shift in philosophical understanding. What Mary reveals, though, is not a metaphorical birthing of revelation at the end of trial and struggle, the *telos* or end result with which Christians tend to encourage one another in times of crisis. Rather, Mary realizes a literal birthing of the ultimate revelation through screams of pain and the shedding of her own blood. Her skin and muscles were stretched and torn as the child emerged, still connected to her as life source until the cord was cut and their mingled blood splattered and the child was separate, distinct, crying and needy. This child, so common in his vulnerability, so near to death, never rose above and overcame that vulnerability. He never attempted to grasp the power to avenge the deaths of the innocent children three and under who were killed in an attempt to extinguish him. Rather, as the Apostle Paul put it, he "learned obedience" and was "made perfect" not in the philosophical teachings of the Sermon on the Mount but "from what he suffered."[3] He was made perfect through his acceptance of the physically horrible limitations given to him, including the limitation of the cross.

We all participate in the grotesquely limited, near-death experience of the beginning of life, and we all remain thusly limited on the brink of death no matter how much our cultural imperatives insist on limitless possibility. Modern, Western thought has wrongly enshrined Mary's story as that of a poor, unwed girl overcoming all the odds and accomplishing the greatest of feats. Her story is rather that of a mother who had sleepless nights; one who agonized over her son being lost; one who sacrificed to raise him only to watch him suffer the most humiliating and painful death possible. Yet, it is this grotesque weakness, even this ultimate limitation of his death, that *realizes* God—that allows God to be known. Again, I do not mean that in weakness God is realized as an aesthetic process of the mind. Essential to Christian belief is not that God was metaphorically made real, but that God was physically made real. And it is also when we live into our own vulnerability that we allow others and God to know us.

The philosophical opposite of a theology of weakness is the survival of the fittest philosophy that arises out of an Enlightened perspective. There is a great line in O'Connor's story "The Life You Save May Be Your Own" that gets to the heart of this dichotomy between modern, scientific ways of knowing and truly being known. When the one-armed Mr. Shiftlet first arrives on the farm, he makes small talk with Mrs. Crater. After noting the sunset and the broken-down car, he says,

> Lady . . . lemme tell you something. There's one of these doctors in Atlanta that's taken a knife and cut the human heart—the human heart . . . out of a man's chest and held it in his hand . . . and studied it like it was a day-old chicken, and lady . . . he don't know no more about it than you or me."[4]

The line is spoken by a disabled person who is tired of being judged by society as less than human and has come to the farm ready to prove he is as capable as anyone. Mr. Shiftlet understands that he cannot be known by his body parts. Present or missing, his physicality does not fully define him. Later in the same conversation, he "jerks his short arm up as if he could point with it to her house and yard and pump," and tells Mrs. Crater, "there ain't a broken thing on this plantation that I couldn't fix for you, one-arm jackleg or not. I'm a man. I got . . . a moral intelligence!"[5] Mr. Shiftlet at once fights against society's poor perception of the disabled and yet gives into the Enlightenment lie of defining humanity according to capability, a giving-in that proves disastrous for him by the end of the story.

As is the case with many of O'Connor's characters, those who come across as grotesque and/or disabled often articulate the most profound truths. I do not mean simply to equate Mr. Shiftlet's short arm with grotesqueness, though it does function as such for the reader of the story (which is in itself an indictment of the reader's participation in modernity's perception of humans). I also mean he is grotesque in that the end of the story portrays his grotesque morality, despite his claim to moral intelligence. Still his claim is not fully lost. O'Connor's characters most often practice their moral intelligence in diagnosing society's problem, not necessarily in practicing a solution. O'Connor prefers to convince through negation, revealing the falsity of prevailing wisdoms.

After he has been on the farm a couple of days, Mr. Shiftlet's diagnosis of society's problem becomes clearer. When Lucynell's mother is surprised that Mr. Shiftlet has taught Lucynell a word, he explains society to Mrs. Crater, "Mr. Shiftlet said that the trouble with the world was that nobody cared, or stopped and took any trouble. He said he never would have been able to teach Lucynell to say a word if he hadn't cared and stopped long enough."[6] This is a rich statement coming from a one-armed vagrant. It is theology from the margins. One could suggest Mr. Shiftlet knows what it is like to be uncared for and unhelped, and that he has the ability to help Lucynell because of this personal knowledge. Also, the phraseology of "took any trouble," though colloquial, is interesting, suggesting people can take other people's burdens upon themselves. According to Shiftlet, Lucynell's inability to speak is a social problem, not an individual's personal tragedy. Her muteness has at least as much to do with how society treats her as it does with what abilities she was born with or without. Mr. Shiftlet is suggesting the social reality of disability, not just the physical problem to be fixed. Unfortunately, like the Misfit in "A Good Man Is Hard to Find" who understands the issue at stake but cannot accept the solution for himself, Mr. Shiftlet is able to diagnose the base problem of society, yet he abandons Lucynell at the story's end just as all of society has done.

Our understanding of what it means to be human—to be American, Western, Enlightened—excludes and marginalizes those whose limitations are more visible. If the base and most important aspect of being human was understood to be relationality, instead of rationality or ability in general, perhaps we would more often stop and "take trouble" upon ourselves, changing and being changed by those whom society currently marginalizes and excludes. Political correctness often attempts to include the marginalized through legislation, which is important, but legislation misses the ultimate point.[7] Our laws for access will remain non-inclusive as long as we are unable to include the marginalized in friendship, to stop and take the time and the "trouble."

O'Connor's problem with the old lady's compassion in the elevator at Davison's is that the old lady made assumptions based upon a false understanding that the significance of being human rests upon one's abilities. O'Connor knows the purpose of life is not to live a "perfect" and suffering-free existence. The lady's desire for perfection (or lack of crutches) betrays her sentimentality. If the lady knew true compassion, she would not pity O'Connor's suffering but align herself with it. She would take the time and trouble to find out what help is actually needed. O'Connor wrote, "There is a better sense in which [compassion] can be used but seldom is—the sense of being in travail with and for creation in its subjection to vanity. This is a sense which implies a recognition of sin; there is a suffering-with, but one which blunts no edges and makes no excuses."[8] This is the sense of compassion that created the incarnation and caused God to suffer with humanity while making no excuses.

One would be remiss to read this statement from O'Connor and not consider her own travailing with and for creation's subjection to vanity. Certainly the lupus that killed her father, crippled her, and had signed her death sentence embodied such vanity, yet she understood all this as a suffering-with creation, a participation in Christ's suffering as the ultimate subjection to vanity. Rather than perceiving disability, or any other limitation, as abnormal or pitiable, she saw limitation as participation in the life and death of Christ, "Who, being in very nature God, did not consider equality with God something to be grasped, but made himself nothing, taking the very nature of a servant, being made in human likeness. And being found in appearance as a man, he humbled himself and became obedient to death— even death on a cross!"[9] The true compassion that "suffers with" is mysteriously part of God's redemption of the world.[10] When O'Connor writes of accepting one's circumstances, she does not mean a hope for the future or a wait-and-see attitude. She means a physical subjection to God's ordering of the world, no matter how full of vanity it is. Such acceptance is the womb for Immanuel.

This mysterious *realization* of Christ is what O'Connor intimates in her fiction. God-in-limitation is what yanks her readers away from their sentimentality toward the mentally handicapped Bishop in *The Violent Bear It Away* and the socially abandoned Harry Ashfield in "The River," and what draws the reader instead into the mystery of the real death that is the first half of their baptisms. Their deaths, seemingly misguided and easily avoidable, are entirely grotesque. However, their grotesqueness does not forfeit their ability to be the authentic good, the dying to self so necessary for resurrection. "What people don't realize," O'Connor wrote, "is how much religion costs. They think faith is a big electric blanket, when of course it is the cross."[11]

The two greatest sacraments in the Christian faith concern death. The first, communion, reminds the participant of Christ's body broken and blood shed. The second, baptism, participates in Christ's death. Death's centrality in the Christian faith should be remembered when a reader is shocked by death in O'Connor's fiction. The ultimate end result for original sin is death, so O'Connor uses death to wake us up to our common beginning and common end. No matter how limitless modernity has fancied itself, it has not and cannot conquer death.

Paradoxically, the only one who has conquered death is the one who submitted to death, and the only way for humans to conquer death is to join in that submission through baptism.

O'Connor was not afraid of death, and neither is her fiction. Accepting death is the most profound acceptance possible, and the greatest form of purity. Acceptance is Christ in the garden the night before his crucifixion—"Not my will but thine be done." Accepting death goes against our sense of justice and our hope for self-sufficiency. To accept death is to accept that something is wrong with the world and to admit our vulnerability. The Christian is taught to make such acceptance a habit, to die to self daily, and baptism acts as an initiation into dying.

Baptizing Modernity in "The River" and The Violent Bear It Away

O'Connor wrote that "if you live today you breathe in nihilism. In or out of the Church, it's the gas you breathe. If I hadn't had the Church to fight it with or to tell me the necessity of fighting it, I would be the stinkingest logical positivist you ever saw right now."[12] O'Connor's affinity for reason allowed her to expose modernity from the inside. Her peculiar gift was to reveal the cosmic struggle between nihilism and divine mystery within the everyday lives of her simple characters. Unveiling the supposed "good" of country people, she reveals all the "isms" of modernity and shows how they are all rooted in the basic philosophy of the Enlightenment, which attempts to attain an ideal form.

While many of her stories are content to reveal the great modern deception, some of her stories disclose what she believed was the answer to the Enlightenment's version of original sin. Her fictional explorations of the sacrament of baptism set this modern incarnation of original sin in the sharpest contrast with the all-demanding requirements of the gospel's answer to human transgression. The first step is the first half of baptism, the going down into death. Any realization of the resurrection in her story "The River" or her second novel, *The Violent Bear It Away*, any hint at the rising out of the water with new life that baptism elicits, is secondary. O'Connor's concern is drowning modernity, the violent and necessary death of self (and self-sufficiency) necessary before participation in Christ's resurrection.

In both "The River" and *The Violent Bear It Away*, her embodiment of baptism occurs in the drowning of an innocent child. In "The River," Harry Ashfield lives in an apartment in a city that is bohemian in its modernity. The reader's only introduction to his parents centers on their having friends over for parties that last well into the night. He wakes each weekend morning to a home predictable in its lack of assistance to him. He does not wake early, but the apartment is "still dark" with drawn shades, and he knows not to disturb his parents. He instead scrounges two crackers spread with anchovy paste left on the coffee table from the night before. He then finds some raisin bread heels and some chocolate milk in the kitchen and inspects the contents of the fridge, where only shriveled vegetables, brown oranges, and a few ingredients for cocktail appetizers are found. Though only four or five years old, Harry has learned the essential element of modern philosophy: self-sufficiency. He figures his parents "would be out cold until one o'clock and that they would all have to go to a restaurant for lunch."[13] Until then, he returns to the living room and entertains himself by dumping out over-flowing ashtrays and carefully smearing the contents into the rug, an apt metaphor for the very modern family in which he abides: the Ashfields.

Lying on the floor, he begins to think about the day before, when his sitter took him to hear a preacher down at the river. The preacher had told him, "If I Baptize you . . . you'll be able to go to the Kingdom of Christ. You'll be washed in the river of suffering, son, and you'll go by the deep river of life." Harry had thought at the time, "I won't go back to the apartment then, I'll go under the river."[14] The preacher baptized Harry and told the boy he counted now and that he did not even count before. Lying in his apartment the next day in the resulting wasteland of his parents' modern lifestyle, Harry understands the preacher's words that he did not count before, and he longs for a connection to something beyond what his parents have offered. "Very slowly, his expression changed as if he were gradually seeing appear what he didn't know he'd been looking for. Then all of a sudden he knew what he wanted to do."[15] He sneaks out of the apartment and returns to the river. He intends "not to fool with preachers any more but to Baptize himself and to keep on going this time until he found the Kingdom of Christ in the river."[16] He accomplishes his goal of baptizing himself and in the story's ending scene, he has disappeared under the river's ripples.

In Ralph Wood's "The Scandalous Baptism of Harry Ashfield," he helpfully relates the story of teaching "The River" to undergraduate students who inevitably perceive the river preacher and Harry's babysitter as the true malefactors of the story. The students argue that the "fundamentalist preacher and fellow believer had practiced the ultimate deceit upon little Harry: they have made him believe that his life's significance lies beyond life. Thus they have engendered the child's needless, indeed meaningless death."[17] The students' reaction is, of course, precisely the scandal O'Connor meant to provoke. Her audience must choose whether the preacher's words about eternal life are a trick or the truth.

The choice is between two ways of being, which are reflected in the two worlds O'Connor creates, that of the Ashfields and that of the sitter.[18] The home in the city, full of art and parties, is mechanical and dead, while the other home, at the edge of town with only two rooms and multiple children, brims with being and mystery. Harry's escape from one life and literal diving into the other is pure in its intention. In his ashy home, nothing seems to count, including him. On the outskirts of the city, though, is a home and a river overflowing with mystic significance.

Wood's students have rightly been disturbed by the story. Harry's death is terribly grotesque. There is no reasonable argument that allows the reader to bypass the grotesqueness of humanity's shared fate. Sentimentally appreciating his escape from a neglectful home environment or even affirming his acceptance of religion is unacceptable. He dies in his search for truth, but the reader cannot afford to respond with an "Awww . . . poor child." The question with which the reader must wrestle is whether or not Harry found truth and whether or not that truth is worth dying for. No matter the reader's answer, the death of Harry remains tragic and grotesque. Religion does not make his death beautiful, but one may be able to accept his death because of religion.

The ending of "The River" leaves the reader bobbing along beside Harry beneath the surface of the river. Inasmuch as the reader pities and has become attached to Harry, the reader feels the suffocation the boy finally embraces, and the reader must also decide if acceptance is the answer. The reader is thus confronted with the question of whether Harry is in a better place when he is lifted by modern philosophies and technologies high above the earth in his New York apartment, or when he is submerged beneath the river of baptism, unable to breathe. If there is something real and true about this baptism, which O'Connor makes every effort to suggest, then a small child's eternal life has been redeemed. As significantly, all modernity has been implicated as that from which the child needed redemption. The only response to modernity's self-sufficiency, O'Connor shouts at us, is death. Wood's students had hold of something truly grotesque, but they got hold of the wrong grotesque by prioritizing physical life over spiritual life and condemning physical death rather than spiritual death.

"The River" is another example of O'Connor's work that focuses on the recognition of original sin, specifically its appearance in modern life encased in Enlightenment idealism. In the story, baptism works as a metaphor for the need to put to death our modern ways of being in the world. The same metaphor holds true for the larger canon of her work. In most of her stories, the characters suffer the (often violent) "drowning" of their original sin. Julian's heart is ripped apart as he realizes he is implicated in his mother's death in "Everything That Rises Must

Converge." Likewise, the end of "The Displaced Person" finds its characters encircling the DP with their implications in his death. In "The Lame Shall Enter First," Sheppard's investment in Rufus and modern psychology is drowned by his son's suicidal "launch into space" in the attic. In all three of these stories, as with "The River," readers are left in the final scene to figure their own implication in these deaths. The reader must ask: How did I view the DP? Did I agree with Sheppard? Am I relieved for Harry? Mrs. Turpin likewise has her original sin drowned by the revelation that is violently forced upon her in the doctor's office and then grows inside her for the rest of the story. The list goes on, and in every instance the reader must question whether he or she helped pull the Misfit's trigger as the gun shot the annoying the grandmother.

The killing of self is the aspect of O'Connor's work encapsulated by her statement that "most of us have learned to be dispassionate about evil, to look it in the face and find, as often as not, our own grinning reflections with which we do not argue."[19] The grotesque-as-evil is the part of her work that shouts to the nearly deaf and draws large and startling figures for the almost blind. The changed perspective O'Connor discusses in her "Introduction to *A Memoir of Mary Ann*" comes across more strongly in her later work. We will be helped in moving forward to remember her words: "But good is another matter. Few have stared at that long enough to accept the fact that its face too is grotesque, that in us the good is something under construction. The modes of evil usually receive worthy expression. The modes of good have to be satisfied with a cliché or a smoothing-down that will soften their real look."[20]

The grotesque-as-good perspective is also in her early work, though often only hinted at. In "The River," for example, the reader readily recognizes and even identifies with the emptiness of the evil that is the Ashfields' apartment. Harry's baptism by the preacher could have served as an apt metaphor for the possible imbuing of eternal life. O'Connor could have sentimentalized the story (surely making Wood's students very happy in the process) by having young Harry return to his apartment after his first baptism with a new joy, a light shining in the darkness of modernity. Instead, she has Harry return to the river by himself and drown himself in "the River of life." In so doing, she challenges the reader to look long enough at the good of baptism and realize that its face too is grotesque, for it is participation in Christ's death. The baptism-as-metaphor that Christianity, particularly evangelical Christianity, generally expresses is really a "smoothing-down that will soften" the real look of the authentic good. Scriptural baptism is willingness to enter martyrdom; true baptism is an unequivocal placing of the spiritual life above the physical, an inversion Wood's students, and many of O'Connor's readers, continually find grotesque.

The Violent Bear It Away

In her mature work, O'Connor goes beyond only hinting at the grotesque good and does more to develop a grotesque expression of the authentic good. Parker's tattoo in "Parker's Back" is a good example of this change.[21] The focus here, though, will be on two of O'Connor's stories whose climactic scene is the drowning by baptism of an innocent child: her novel *The Violent Bear It Away* (*TVBIA*). In *TVBIA* we find some recognizable characters. Tarwater is running from his calling to be a prophet, and his journey takes many of the same turns Hazel Motes took in O'Connor's first novel. Bishop's father, Rayber, is another Sheppard,[22] the penultimate modern man complete with degrees and psychological insights. And Bishop is the innocent child who is overwhelmed by the story's action, as is the case with Lucynell Crater and Harry Ashfield.

The novel begins with young Tarwater digging a grave for his great-uncle Mason Tarwater. Mason kidnapped young Tarwater away from his uncle Rayber shortly after Tarwater's parents died. He raised the child in the backwoods, teaching him "Figures, Reading, Writing, and History beginning with Adam expelled from the Garden and going on down through the presidents to Herbert Hoover and on in speculation toward the Second

Coming and the Day of Judgment."[23] Mason also instructed him in the ways of prophecy and the terrible suffering and obedience necessary for being God's prophet. As the old man neared death, he made sure Tarwater knew to do two things after his demise: the boy must bury his body "deep enough so the dogs wouldn't be able to dig him up," and he must baptize his idiot cousin Bishop.

Once the old man dies, Tarwater obediently begins to dig a grave. Soon, though, he gets a taste of the freedom every child experiences when first separated from parental authority. "Now I can do anything I want to . . . I could kill off those chickens if I wanted to."[24] Tarwater begins hearing demonic whisperings that lead him further and further in rebellion away from Mason and concern for anyone other than himself. His movement from acceptance of his given life through the freedom of autonomy in creating his own self to the killing of the socially insignificant Bishop is a reiteration of O'Connor's prophetic warning that modernity's insistence on autonomy leads to the creation of gas chambers.

Tarwater initially rejects the voice of this demonic friend but rapidly succumbs to its reasonableness and is soon violently rejecting his calling instead. The "freedom" he found in not having to obey Mason when he was tired of digging the grave shortly transforms into a necessarily absolute rejection of authority.[25] He finds he *must* do the opposite of what Mason told him, so he sets the farmhouse ablaze in order to burn Mason's body and then sets out to live with and learn from the very embodiment of all that Mason stood against as a prophet: Tarwater's uncle Rayber. Finally, to rid himself of any possibility of ever fulfilling his prophetic duty of baptism, he purposes to kill his cousin Bishop.

The prophet's caller, however, thwarts his will (and the will of the evil one speaking to Tarwater). After setting the house on fire, Tarwater makes his way to the city to find his uncle Rayber and learn how to be "normal." But he finds he is unable to learn anything from his uncle. Later, when he drowns his cousin

Bishop, he begins pronouncing the words of baptism over him, thereby bestowing the sacrament unto eternal salvation in his murderous act. Finally, when he returns to the house he burnt, someone has dragged Mason's body out before the blaze and given it a proper Christian burial in the grave Tarwater had begun to dig.

Tarwater is never able to get Mason's words of prophetic calling out of his head. "The prophet is coming with the Lord's message. 'Go warn the children of God,' saith the Lord, 'of the terrible speed of justice.' Who will be left? Who will be left when the Lord's mercy strikes?"[26] In O'Connor's vision, God's refusing to be silenced or turned aside by rejection *is* God's mercy, even when mercy must strike violently in order to be made known. The violence of mercy is the paradox of God's grace. The violence of mercy is O'Connor's own lupus. It is Mary Ann with the cancerous tumor on her face. It is the children with Down syndrome whose birth O'Connor predicted our society would find a way to disallow.

O'Connor understood that rather than "evil" being "a problem to be solved," as modernism has decreed, it is "a mystery to be endured."[27] Human nature wants to join in the fight, to identify evil and join God in battle against it. The problem, O'Connor shows again and again, is that we consistently misidentify evil. We think pleasure or accomplishment or some sentimental caring for others will make us good and pure of heart, and we equate suffering, or what we deem suffering, to be the greatest evil. As Mason sums it up in a rage of prophecy and one of my favorite O'Connor lines, "Ignore the Lord Jesus as long as you can! Spit out the bread of life and sicken on honey!"[28]

Tarwater's uncle Rayber embodies modernity's misguided search to avoid suffering, and the end result is that he says concerning his own son Bishop, "In a hundred years people may have learned enough to put them to sleep when they're born."[29] It has taken less than a hundred years, and prenatal testing in which "suffering" is predicted and subsequently terminated is now common practice. When we misidentify evil, we end up fighting against what is God's mercy to us, and we participate in crucifying Christ rather than participating in his suffering.

In *TVBIA*, O'Connor reveals mercy-as-grotesque more clearly than in any of her other writings.[30] She links God's beauty, love, and awe—Otto's "numinous"[31]—with the "idiot prophet" Mason and the "idiot child" Bishop. To see this connection plainly, the reader is invited to view Mason and Bishop through the eyes of the unredeemed Rayber, whose thorough-going modernism finds no use for either. In Rayber's son Bishop, in particular, the grotesque and the holy become one. Rayber is satisfied to explain Mason's radical religiosity by employing psychological analysis, as when he wrote an article about his uncle noting, "His fixation of being called by the Lord had its origin in insecurity. He needed the assurance of a call, and so he called himself."[32] Rayber cannot, however, explain Bishop's idiocy.

Rayber had also been kidnapped and trained by Mason when he was young, but only for four days. Rayber completely rejected Mason's teachings and went as far as possible in the opposite direction, embracing modernism. Rather than being a prophet, he became a school psychologist, an anti-prophet calling himself to the mission of spreading the gospel of self-reliance. He proclaims a "natural" salvation "through your own efforts. Your intelligence."[33] Again parroting modernism, he declares, "If there's any way to be born again, it's a way that you accomplish yourself, an understanding about yourself that you reach after a long time, perhaps a long effort. It's nothing you get from above by spilling a little water and a few words."[34] Having a developmentally disabled child, though, calls all of his philosophy into question. His philosophical stance demands that the child, unable to accomplish for himself, is useless, and yet love for the child continues to well up within him, unreasonable and *purpose*less love.

Bishop is most often referred to in the novel as the "idiot child," lacking as he does the intelligence necessary for Rayber's form of salvation. The reader meets Bishop on Tarwater's first trip to the city, which occurred before Mason's death. Mason and Tarwater arrive at Rayber and Bishop's apartment, where Mason intends to baptize Bishop. When the door opens, "A small pink-faced boy [stands] in it with his mouth hung in a silly smile. . . . He [is] gnawing on a brown apple core." Bishop makes "an unintelligible noise" and shuts the door. Mason turns and tells Tarwater, "He don't have good sense."[35] The scene's action then shifts to a confrontation between Mason and Rayber. When Rayber comes to the door, Mason exclaims, "The Lord Jesus Christ sent me to baptize that boy! . . . Stand aside. I mean to do it!" He also claims, "That boy cries out for his baptism," and "Precious in the sight of the Lord even an idiot!" Rayber, however, refuses and tells Mason to get off his property: "If you don't I'll have you put back in the asylum where you belong." The confrontation escalates until both are shouting, and Rayber says, "You get away from here! . . . Ask the Lord why He made him an idiot in the first place, uncle. Tell him I want to know why!"[36]

Since Rayber's philosophy centers on self-sufficiency, he sees no point in the child's existence, for the child cannot even care for himself, much less add anything productive to society. In contrast to Mason's view of Bishop as precious in God's sight and his affirmation of the boy's own participation in salvation ("That boy cries out for his baptism"), Rayber responds, "You could slosh water on him for the rest of his life and he'd still be an idiot. Five years old for all eternity, useless forever. . . . he'll never be baptized—just as a matter of principle, nothing else. As a gesture of human dignity, he'll never be baptized."[37] Unfortunately Rayber's view of Bishop as "useless forever" remains a far too familiar sentiment toward the developmentally disabled even fifty years later.[38]

Ever since his own baptism in the woods at the hands of Mason, Rayber has turned to modern philosophy and psychology to explain away his uncle's insanity, even having his uncle committed to the asylum at one time. He views Mason and Bishop through the same lens of modernity, and they both fall short of what he understands it means to be a modern man.[39] O'Connor links Bishop and Mason together in the novel by having Rayber use the word idiot for both of them and by consistently referring to what does and does not make "sense." For Rayber, an idiot is the opposite of rational, and the goal and purpose of humanity is to rationally understand everything so it can be made better.

Tarwater's internal struggle is the same as Rayber's. The voice in his head tries to convince him that his great uncle Mason was just crazy and that if he follows after Mason, he will also be crazy. Early on the voice sets up a dichotomy between reason and belief, telling Tarwater, " 'The trouble with you, I see,' he concluded, 'is that you ain't got but just enough sense to believe every word he told you.' "[40] Mason says the trouble with Rayber is the exact opposite: "He don't know it's anything he can't know . . . That's his trouble."[41] So the stage has been set between Rayber (and modernity) trying to know everything, and Mason (and O'Connor) believing in what they cannot know. The plot concerns which voice Tarwater will choose to follow, and ultimately which voice Rayber will find sustainable. Will Rayber and Tarwater give into the idiocy of religion and love or stand against it, protecting themselves from it with all the machinery of modern reason?

Though Tarwater attempts to flee to his uncle to learn how to be a modern man and escape his prophetic upbringing at the hands of Mason,[42] he ultimately finds Rayber's vision to be exactly what Mason had told him: Rayber can only *think* and is unable to *do*.[43] This split within Rayber is forced to the surface in his relationship with his son. In spite of all the psychological explanation he is able to give for Mason's religious idiocy, the narrator notes Rayber "had not conquered the problem of Bishop. He had only learned to live with it and had learned too that he could not live without it."[44] As much as Rayber desires to view Bishop as a problem to be solved, an x needing an answer, Bishop remains an unbearable enigma. Rayber cannot escape a "horrifying love" for the child that, if he is not careful to hold in check, becomes "so outrageous that he would be left shocked and depressed for days, and trembling for his sanity."[45] This love for Bishop is Rayber's inescapable entry point into a love of and for all creation, a love that begins with Bishop but infuses the whole world. The novel's narrator explains the tension within Rayber:

> His normal way of looking on Bishop was as an *x* signifying the general hideousness of fate. He did not believe that he himself was formed in the image and likeness of God but that Bishop was he had no doubt. The little boy was part of a simple equation that required no further solution, except at the moments when with little or no warning he would feel himself overwhelmed by the horrifying love. Anything he looked at too long could bring it on. Bishop did not have to be around. It could be a stick or a stone, the line of a shadow, the absurd old man's walk of a starling crossing the sidewalk. If, without thinking, he lent himself to it, he would feel suddenly a morbid surge of the love that terrified him—powerful enough to throw him to the ground in an act of idiot praise. It was completely irrational and abnormal.[46]

We see here again Rayber's understanding that normal things correspond to rationality and anything irrational is abnormal. The end result of modern philosophy has so isolated him that he finds the feeling of love abnormal because it is irrational. Rayber knows that Bishop is made in God's image, and he sees that this makes both Bishop and God abnormal, irrational, and useless. We also see, however, that something as irrational and idiotic as praise is just below the surface even of this most modern man.

The quoted paragraph's reference to the *imago Dei* is placed in juxtaposition on one side to Rayber's mathematical view of Bishop and on the other side to Rayber's uncontrollable love for Bishop. The reference to Bishop being in the image of God can thus be interpreted in quite different directions. Prioritizing the *imago Dei*'s juxtaposition to the following sentences about Rayber's love recognizes Bishop as the source of a love that flows from God into all of creation. In this view, Bishop is "the locus of the sacred" in the novel and "represents the divine mystery."[47] The problem with this analysis is that it ignores the statement that precedes the image of God reference, the statement that says Rayber views Bishop as "an *x* signifying the general hideousness of fate."

On the other hand, since Rayber views Bishop as signifying the hideousness of fate, one can interpret Rayber's naming

Bishop as being in the image of God as Rayber's sarcastic view of God, a God who is made in the image of the imbecilic Bishop.[48] A sarcastic interpretation fits well with a good majority of Rayber's philosophy. However, it does not do justice to Rayber's "horrifying love" for Bishop.

For O'Connor, both are true simultaneously. Whereas much of O'Connor's early work included only the grotesque-as-metaphor for original sin, in *TVBIA* O'Connor uses the grotesque to point in both directions at once. As often as not, she seems to say that the grotesque is the authentic good, and our inability to perceive it as good signifies how truly we are overcome by original sin. O'Connor quite purposefully sandwiched the *imago Dei* reference between the modern "God is dead" perspective that corresponds to Rayber's "normal way of looking on Bishop as an *x*" and the orthodox Christian perspective that humans are made in the image of a God whose love is "powerful enough to throw him to the ground in an act of idiot praise." O'Connor refuses an either/or dichotomy and instead opens her readers to the mystery of a both/and. For the unredeemed, cynical, modern man that Rayber is, Bishop's developmental disability serves as proof of God's nonexistence—or perhaps God's developmentally disabled existence. Yet, the love that results from relationship with Bishop, a love untethered to any modern notion of purpose or productivity, spreads over even the most antireligious person. Thus an emphasis on Bishop as the locus of the sacred is also correct.

In the paragraph following the one quoted above, O'Connor explores further the purposelessness of the unavoidable love Rayber has for Bishop, a purposelessness that fully defies Rayber's Enlightenment thinking.

> He was not afraid of love in general. He knew the value of it and how it could be used. He had seen it transform in cases where nothing else had worked, such as with his poor sister. None of this had the least bearing on his situation. The love that would overcome him was of a different order entirely. It was not the kind that could be used for the child's improvement or his own. It was love without reason, love for something futureless, love that appeared to exist only to be itself,

imperious and all demanding, the kind that would cause him to make
a fool of himself in an instant. And it only began with Bishop. It began
with Bishop and then like an avalanche covered everything his reason
hated.[49]

There is, I suggest, no fuller expression of the good in O'Connor's
work than what she embodies in Bishop and in Rayber's relationship with him. This love is not the opposite of reason, but
neither is it congruent with reason, and it is certainly more powerful than reason. It is a love that hounds a person, overwhelm-
ing him or her, and only a person's most adamant refusals of this
love are able to hold it at bay, and that only at the cost of being
"shocked and depressed for days, and trembling for his sanity."[50]
To a society based on reason, this love is grotesque, shocking,
even depressing and sanity-threatening. This love is also, however, the authentic good. It is the same grotesque and sanity-
threatening love that places a savior on a cross.

Bishop's mental disability prohibits the purposeful love
Rayber is willing to accept. Society's understanding of what it
means to be a human, a citizen, has difficulty including people
like Bishop. What *TVBIA* suggests in contrast to modernity is
a love that has its origin in God and infuses creation on the
grounds of being and mystery, not function and reason. This love
inhabits all people and even all of creation with its purposeless
significance, a significance Bishop is better able to reveal precisely because of his disability.

The positive connection O'Connor makes between the idiocy of religion and the developmentally disabled is profound.
From Rayber's perspective, both religion and the developmentally disabled are unreasonable and useless. From O'Connor's
perspective, however, reasonability or usefulness cannot define
being. We were not created to accomplish, but to be and to be in
relationship.[51] Love in action, O'Connor shows, always trumps
the actless good intentions that fill Rayber and modernity, but
ultimately sit by while a human being is drowned.

Mason regularly references Bishop's idiocy as his protection
from disbelief. According to Mason, God preserved Bishop from

Rayber's modern reason "in the only possible way: the child was dim-witted."[52] In other words, Bishop is saved from the Enlightenment's overemphasis on reason by not having reason.[53] Bishop demands community and engenders a horrifying love, horrifying because of its mysterious origin unaffiliated with anything reasonable, and horrifying because of the demands it makes on Rayber's self-sufficiency. Bishop, then, is not only protected from Rayber's modernity, as Mason suggests, but he is also the key for Rayber to escape modernity's empty, reason-only promises. The grotesque Bishop is Rayber's call (and modernity's call) to define being human by relationship rather than reason, by vulnerability rather than self-sufficiency. Unfortunately Rayber refuses the call as he sits on the shore of the lake at the end of the story and listens to the drowning of his son Bishop.

In "The River" the reader is invited to view the all-demanding reality of baptism from the perspective of a four- or five-year-old child who chooses baptism-as-meaning. Harry Ashfield chooses to die to the ashfields of his life and to be alive somewhere where he counts. Everything about Harry's story is grotesque, but the reader must choose if one of these grotesques is actually the authentic good. In *The Violent Bear It Away*, the reader is invited to view baptism from the perspective of modernity. The modern perspective finds uselessness meaningless and is not only blind to humanity's search for meaning, as is the case for Sheppard concerning his son's suicide, but participates in the murder of anything or anyone that does not serve its purposes. Rayber and Bishop's story is also grotesque, indeed horrifying. Again, though, the reader must choose if Rayber has participated in killing the authentic good in his life, if in being "busy cutting down human imperfection," he has been "making headway also on the raw material of good."[54]

CHAPTER 4

The Image of Christ and a Disability Perspective

"I read a lot of theology because it makes my writing bolder."

—Flannery O'Connor[1]

In Luke 19, Jesus enters Jerusalem on a donkey a week before his crucifixion. The author did not have to tell his readers that Jesus' action was in fulfillment of prophecy. They knew. Jesus' disciples, the Twelve and the others following him on that day, knew as well. Their desire for the promised Messiah ran deep; their longing for freedom from oppressors was tangible. As Jesus approached the path that led down the Mount of Olives, "the whole multitude of the disciples began to praise God joyfully with a loud voice." They shouted, "Blessed is the king who comes in the name of the Lord! Peace in heaven and glory in the highest heaven."[2] As Jesus rode the donkey across the tiny Kidron Valley and started up the path, only a few hundred yards, to enter Jerusalem's city gate, the expectations for Jesus-as-king were high, so high that the Pharisees in the crowd perceived a danger and warned Jesus to have his disciples be quiet. The Romans atop the city walls that they were approaching might be inclined quickly to crush any sign of a political uprising.

For many centuries, Christians have celebrated this triumphant entry on Palm Sunday for good reason. The people had
finally realized Jesus' true identity as the Anointed One (Christ
in Greek, Messiah in Hebrew). Luke draws a beautiful picture
of this multitude shouting for their king. Matthew's version has
the participants waving palm branches and laying their coats
on the road in honor of their realized messiah. Luke provides
us with a further insight, though; he knows the multitude has
not truly understood. They have not realized that "the face of
the good is also grotesque" and only "half full of promise." The
gospel accounts are full of the irony of the scene that some of
these same people would be crying out for Jesus' death only a
few days later.

But Luke helps the reader glimpse a deeper paradox. As
Jesus approached the city, "he wept over it."[3] During his own
triumphant entry, amidst the shouts of realization of his true
identity, Jesus wept. And he said, "If you, even you, had only recognized on this day the things that make for peace! But they are
hidden from your eyes."[4] The scene's paradox is that the humiliation of the cross is the thing that makes for the peace these disciples cry out for in expectation. They will have to learn to accept
Christ's death before they can know the peace they desperately
anticipate. They cry for a king and for "Peace in heaven," but
Christ says they do not know "the things that make for peace."
Jesus weeps because the people do not understand this paradox.
Despite years of teaching, they still cannot comprehend that the
face of the good is grotesque.

O'Connor's fiction captures the mystery and paradox of this
moment. Amidst our expectations for liberation, our desires to
be justified and for justice to be carried out on our enemies,
O'Connor points us down the *via dolorosa*. Our sense of justice
is offended and our hearts are crushed when the innocent boys
Harry and Bishop are drowned in their baptisms. But have we
seen the things that make for peace? We want our religion to
be a big electric blanket, but O'Connor continually points us
toward the Cross.[5]

O'Connor's Image of Christ

If Christ is the true image of God, then radical questions have to be asked about the nature of the God who is imaged. At the heart of Christian theology is a critique of success, power and perfection, and an honouring of weakness, brokenness and vulnerability.

—Ecumenical Disabilities Advocate Network
of the World Council of Churches,
"A Church of All and For All"

O'Connor's image of Christ drove her fiction. But her image of Christ was not the victorious and conquering king the Jews of Jesus' day and the Christians of O'Connor's day (or our day) expected. Hers was instead the image of Christ on the cross that was installed above the altar at Milledgeville's Sacred Heart Catholic Church in the 1930s.[6] O'Connor's practice was to attend mass every morning, and she surely spent a good deal of time over the years reflecting on that cross. Certainly she believed in an eventual, victorious kingdom of heaven, but her practical theology was a well-developed theology of God as co-sufferer. Another way of putting it is to say that the core theme of O'Connor's fiction can be found in how she so closely relates the socially monstrous hermaphrodite in "A Temple of the Holy Ghost" with the raised Monstrance encasing the communion Host, and how she relates both the monstrous and the Monstrance to the embodied working out of salvation in the temple of the Holy Ghost that is the story's unnamed protagonist.

Brad Gooch's biography of O'Connor tells of her resemblance to her father in appearance and "on the inside too." Their love for one another and special bond was obvious to all who knew the family.[7] Her relationship with him provides insight into her faith as well and helps account for her image of Christ. In the first paragraph of a 1956 letter, O'Connor wrote to Betty Hester about her view of God: "I've never spent much time over the bride-bridegroom analogy. For me, perhaps because it began for me in the beginning, it's been more father and child." Her following sentence shifts the focus but only to clarify the picture: "The things you have said about my being surprised to be over twelve, etc., have struck me as being quite comically accurate."[8] O'Connor's faith was the deep trust of a child sitting in the lap of her father. Saying she had childlike faith, though, does not imply simplicity, for her faith was deeply intertwined with the tremendous longing and pain that she came to know as her father died rather suddenly of lupus when she was only fifteen.

O'Connor began the second paragraph of the above-mentioned letter with a quote she had recently found: "Nobody would have paid any attention to Jesus if he hadn't been a martyr but had died at the age of eighty of athlete's foot."[9] At the center of the formation of O'Connor's faith lay the event of her father's death and a profound sense of Christ's sacrifice on the cross. One might expect a typical teenager to have rebelled against a God who would allow such horrible things to happen to good people. O'Connor seems to have instead fallen more deeply into her faith, finding strength and comfort there, so much so that only a decade later she rather gracefully accepted her own death sentence by the very same disease.

Of the annoying grandmother in "A Good Man is Hard to Find," the Misfit says, "She would of been a good woman . . . if it had been somebody there to shoot her every minute of her life."[10] Lupus was the Misfit's gun in O'Connor's life, and examining her response to this gun can teach us some important lessons about being good. The first thing we learn from O'Connor is that we have misidentified the good, thinking the good is the lack of a gun, the lack of suffering. The Enlightenment taught us that suffering equals evil. We are shocked that the grandmother's entire family is so callously killed in the story, and we pity O'Connor's struggle with lupus. For O'Connor, though, a gun is already and always pointed at us all, whether justified or not. The gun of lupus shot her father, and she lived with it pressed against her side. Her acceptance of this death sentence is a great mystery that she inhabited quite naturally. For her, the true good is not the lack of suffering, but how we react when we finally realize a gun is pointed at us. The grandmother reached out to touch the Misfit, her killer. And O'Connor asks us, can we reach out to embrace the very world—the very misfit people or mis-fit justice—that will kill us? O'Connor did. She embraced the limitations lupus caused in her life, and she found them to be gateways to something more real. Such an embrace and accep-tance is the mystery of the incarnation, Christ embracing those who would kill him, and becomes the mystery of how we are transformed into the likeness of Christ as we embrace a world full of death.

A journal entry from O'Connor's first year of college, about four years after her father's death and five years before her diag-nosis, reads,

> The reality of death has come upon us and a consciousness of the power of God has broken our complacency like a bullet in the side. A sense of the dramatic, of the tragic, of the infinite, has descended upon us, filling us with grief, but even above grief, wonder. Our plans were so beautifully laid out, ready to be carried to action, but with magnificent certainty God laid them aside and said, "You have forgotten—mine?"[11]

Death for O'Connor, specifically her father's death, felt like a bullet in the side, a pain that connected her to Christ's death and the spear in his side. Like the disciples in Luke crying out for the Messiah during the triumphal entry, we have our plans beautifully laid out. But Christ weeps and asks if we have for-gotten God's plan.

O'Connor's faith was a profound mixture of the reverent awe she had for God, a child sitting in her father's lap, and the divine violence that she felt accompanies the carrying out of God's will within a fallen world. She knew firsthand the pain of a cosmically fallen world that would take the life of an innocent Jesus as well as the life of her father. These are the same deaths as the drowning of the innocent Harry Bevel and Bishop. The dramatic, the tragic, and the infinite are all intertwined in her vision and descend upon us all at once, indistinguishable from one another, engendering both grief and wonder. Our wrestling with this mixture of grief and wonder in her fiction creates the mystery that is the aim and purpose of her writing and is the reality of the life she lived.

O'Connor does not simply tell her readers of this mystery, for the mystery cannot be told. The mystery of Christ's salvation is not *told* in the Sermon on the Mount. The mystery resides in God taking on flesh and dying for the sake of the world. Christ had to live out the mystery of suffering, *embodying* it, and so did O'Connor, and so do we. As she learned to accept the death lupus brought her father and the disability lupus created for her, lupus became her opportunity to share in the sufferings of Christ in order also to share in Christ's resurrection; her limitations became the gateway to the truest realities of her religion. Lupus was her cross, and she wrestled with it daily in the garden of Gethsemane, and it seems most days she at least conceded "Not my will but thine," thus accepting the violence that bears away the kingdom of heaven. Hers was a theology forged in the fires of pain and suffering, a theology that lived the incomprehensible mystery of the Apostle Paul's words from Colossians: "In my flesh I am completing what is lacking in Christ's afflictions for the sake of his body, that is, the church."[12]

A Theology of Disability

O'Connor's sense of mystery, so central to her purpose in writing, flowed from her struggle with disability. In fact, we can reference her perspective as a theology of disability, with "of" connoting "from," not "for." [13] Much as O'Connor's voice was as one crying in the wilderness, demanding modernity's repentance, her voice was also as one crying in the wilderness and preparing the way for a disability perspective. In recent years, more voices with a similar message have begun to be heard. These similar voices, also arising from a struggle with and embrace of disability, focus on the two subjects that come across most potently in O'Connor's life and fiction: an attack on Enlightenment ways of defining humanity and an incarnational embrace of human limitation. A theology of disability tends to take as its starting point a particular embodiment of humanity, such as a family member with Down syndrome or one's own physical limitations, and beginning with that particularity considers theology and the world from the perspective that all people are limited, instead of from the Enlightenment ideal of a perfect body toward which we should all strive.

As noted in the discussion of the significance of limitation for O'Connor, the Enlightenment perspective has reached its cultural pinnacle in the medical field and its theological pinnacle in the prosperity gospel, both of which a theology of disability strongly critiques. The medical model myopically views only the body, and only the individual, both being end results of Enlightenment philosophy.[14] Medicine's goal is to rehabilitate persons with disabilities, to make them "normal" so they can reenter society as productive members. Marvelously, advances in medicine have added a great number of benefits to the lives of the disabled, the greatest of which has been the extension of life itself. The medical model has failed, however, in addressing persons as whole human beings and addressing social factors that create, sustain, or enlarge disability. The same can be said of the Enlightenment overall.

The medical perspective has also become dominant as society's view of disability, resulting in isolation and shame for persons with disabilities. Since medicine perceives an idealized able body as "normal," a *dis*abled body is abnormal, lacking and in need of a fix, causing disability always and repetitively to be viewed negatively.[15] The perception of disability-as-lack can be traced all the way back to Aristotle's "'generic type' against which all physical variation appears as different, derivative, inferior, and insufficient."[16] Only in modern times, though, has ability defined what it means to be human, and only with modern medicine have humans possessed the power so nearly to separate the dis from ability. However, along with the great feats of medicine, the medical model has simultaneously objectified disabled people as problems to be solved, as patients subservient to the authority of "healing" medicine, and, at its worst, as social deviants in need of separation from or even elimination from society.[17] In the United States, and many other Western countries, the attempt to "fix" disability has been part of a social need to homogenize society for the sake of efficiency, the aim being to make everyone "normal" so that equality can be true in a labor-defined society.[18] Theologically, one can relate the Enlightenment's seeking of perfection to certain Jewish and early Christian attempts to be justified by perfectly keeping the law. The Apostle Paul's response to the confidence of others in the law or perfection of words is to boast in his weakness, a theological concept to which we will return.

In contrast to the medical model's concern for normalizing individuals' bodies, a disability perspective relocates the problem of disability within the larger society.[19] While the medical perspective tries to "fix" an individual's impairment, disability explores how the true impairment is in society's response to disability, not in an individual's inability to be normal and/or productive. An overly simplistic example of the social construction of disability runs along the following lines. If a person needs to get to the fourth floor of a building that has no elevator, and this person is in a wheelchair, she has a very definite disability. However, if the building has an elevator, the person is not un-*able* to get to the fourth floor, thus the person is not *dis*abled. From a disability perspective, the problem is not a matter of physical or mental impotence, but society's limiting who has access. The problem is a moral/ethical prejudging of the abnormal according to socially defined hierarchies based upon physical or mental attributes, attributes which change for all of us throughout our lives. From a disability perspective, the problem to be fixed sits in the middle of society with its inability to accommodate limitations, not in the middle of a wheelchair with its ability to accommodate limitations.

Another overly simplistic, and very different, example will help. In a society built upon, infused with, and empowered by competition and efficiency, persons with profound developmental disabilities are considered highly deficient and disabled. However, if our society were based upon affection or giving, some of these "disabled" people would become our teachers, as Henri Nouwen found at Daybreak and Jean Vanier learned forty years ago when he cofounded the L'Arche communities.[20] As we have seen, O'Connor enfleshes the distance between a disability perspective and an Enlightenment perspective in the relationship between Rayber and his son Bishop in *The Violent Bear It Away*. Rayber finds no purpose in his son's existence, yet his love for Bishop draws him into the mystery of being itself.

Applying a disability perspective to theology changes our very perception of God.[21] Modernity-influenced theology has made God out of the clay of our personal and national ideals. We tend to think of God's attributes as unlimited extensions of our best attributes. We imagine God's power is like ours, except without limitation.[22] Rayber's atheism arises from this very point. As an embodiment of Enlightenment theory, he believes in science's eventual ability to fix all problems. If he currently had all the answers, he would fix all of the problems. A God who supposedly has the ability to "fix" his son, but does not do so, makes no sense to Rayber. When his uncle the prophet comes to baptize Bishop, Rayber shouts at his uncle, "Ask the Lord why He made him an idiot in the first place, uncle. Tell him I want to know why!"[23] Through his relationship with Bishop, Rayber comes to an essential truth about the *imago Dei*. Rayber "did not believe that he himself was formed in the image and likeness of God but that Bishop was he had no doubt."[24] Perceiving God as disabled is, of course, unacceptable for Rayber and his Enlightenment understanding of humanity. A theology of disability, though, posits that viewing God as disabled helps break our tendency to define God according to our constructed definitions of what is best about us. A disabled "image of God jars us out of our tendency to conceive God as 'unlimitedly' able. It reminds us to think of God's power christologically—God's being with us, suffering with us, broken for us."[25] *The Violent Bear It Away* suggests that Rayber is right to perceive Bishop as being made in the image of God. Rayber's "horrifying love" for the boy "was completely irrational and abnormal,"[26] just as God's love is for humans. Rayber's own philosophical stance, though, does not allow him to accept this vision of an irrational, loving God or to accept his irrational, loving son. Thus he participates in the death of his son by purposefully ignoring his drowning, just as he participates in the crucifixion of Christ by purposefully ignoring the cross.

O'Connor's lack of bitterness or complaining about her disability is due to her image of Christ, which did not allow her to expect anything other than suffering. She was as one of the Desert Fathers to whom the mixture of power and Christianity did not make sense. Scripture is clear that God is more powerful than human beings, yet it is not through our understandings of power that the Word became flesh. Rather, it is the power of limitation, humility, vulnerability—a baby is born, fragile and dependent. Likewise, at the end of Christ's mission, the plan for salvation is not one that participates in the principalities and powers of this world, whether political or social. "Jesus on the cross is God disabled, made weak and vulnerable to worldly powers because of the perfection of divine love." This image of the disabled God "reminds us that, from a christological perspective, God's perfection, God's goodness, God's identity are so far from transcending the suffering of the world that they participate deeply and unavoidably in that very suffering."[27] O'Connor understood her own suffering—and the suffering of Mary Ann's tumored face and Betty Hester's loneliness and Mrs. Turpin's forehead and Harry's baptism—as somehow mysteriously participating in a cosmic christological suffering that leads to redemption, at least for those who are able to accept the grotesque good. O'Connor's challenge was confronting a modern perspective that saw no mystery, no meaning in suffering, and felt itself not only capable of eliminating suffering but morally obligated to do so, even at the expense of drowning one's own son or creating mass gas chambers. O'Connor's answer was beautifully similar to the Apostle Paul's boasting in weakness.

Quite counter to cultural and medical understandings of perfection, divine perfection is revealed in the unlimited vulnerability of the incarnation and the cross. The perfection Jesus commands in the Beatitudes, to be perfect as your heavenly Father is perfect,[28] is a perfection born of this vulnerability and dependency, not of self-sufficient legalism or absolute power. Even after resurrection, Christ's body is not conformed to what we would recognize as perfect. He instead appears before the disciples in a disabled body, with stigmata in his hands, feet, and side, and his disability functions as the confirmation of his messianic identity when he invites Thomas to put his hand *in* his side.[29] Christ's scars are no mere scars for the sake of remembering. His is a body forever impaled by the corruptible materials of nails and a spear. The cross was not just suffering for the sake of future perfection. The cross was instead a vision of the true reality that prioritizes as our only means of salvation what we have deemed inferior, despicable, and grotesque. God is so concerned with relationship that God is willing to take the marks of humiliation upon Christ's body for all eternity.

The World Council of Churches' 2003 statement on disability argues similarly. The members interpret the *imago Dei* through soteriology (the study of salvation), which prioritizes the righting of God's relationship with humans, instead of through creation, which tends to focus on human ability or function. The World Council statement argues that it is only in Christ's redemption of the world that we glimpse the true meaning of being made in God's image. As Paul notes in 1 Corinthians 12, in Christ we are all one body and the lesser parts are just as important, and the parts that are shameful are particularly honored. The point of being the body of Christ is not to identify who makes up the brain or the eye and who are the intestines. Paul's point is the relationship between all the parts, the brain's eventual death if the intestines do not absorb the necessary nutrients and flush out the toxins. The World Council centers its argument for a disability perspective on this relationality that is the body of Christ. The members write,

> We would therefore argue that: (1) Christian theology needs to interpret the *imago Dei* from a Christological and soteriological (the saving work of Christ for the world) standpoint, which takes us beyond the usual creationist and anthropological perspectives. (2) Christian theology needs to embrace a non-elitist, inclusive understanding of the body of Christ as the paradigm for understanding the *imago Dei*. (3) Without

the full incorporation of persons who can contribute from the experience of disability, the church falls short of the glory of God, and cannot claim to be in the image of God. Without the insight of those who have experience of disability, some of the most profound and distinctive elements of Christian theology are easily corrupted or lost.[30]

Inasmuch as the revelation of God's love is dependent upon the self-limitation of the incarnation and the disability of the cross, then a modern perspective that attempts to eliminate limitations also attempts to eliminate God's revelation in Christ. A focus on vulnerable communion, though, transforms how we view who we are. Relationships, rather than autonomy, become the goal.[31] Rayber (and the Enlightenment and the medical field) has it backwards. Since Bishop could never be self-sufficient, Rayber found no purpose for him. If Rayber could have prioritized relationship, though, Bishop could have led him deeply into the mysteries of God. He could have learned that the need for love and the possibility for love arise from places of limitation and vulnerability. This is Christ's body broken for us, God's love for the world.

A theology of disability breaks what we have seen as a necessary connection between perfection and power. "To posit a Jesus Christ who needs care and mutuality as essential to human-divine survival does not symbolize either humanity or divinity as powerless. Instead it debunks the myth of individualism and hierarchical orders, in which transcendence means breaking free of encumbrances and needing nobody and constitutes the divine as somebody in relation to other bodies."[32] God was broken for the sake of relationship with broken humanity. Brokenness, however, is not a matter of power or the lack thereof. Power cannot be in any way equated with perfection, as human culture consistently asserts. In God's redemption, the very opposites are true. Christ's perfection comes through his obedience and submission, submission that included the complete brokenness of the cross.

Disability serves theology as "a profound symbol of human brokenness," but also as more than a symbol. When we push away those we consider abnormal and deficient, "we shun what is perhaps most human about us—the need to belong and to be recognized as of value. We all at the core are vulnerable and receive our existence from one another . . . Learning to embrace ourselves and others as we are, in our specific weaknesses, releases us from narcissistic self-enclosure and empowers us to risk the openness of genuine relationship."[33] These genuine relationships make us whole persons, a wholeness achieved not despite vulnerability and disability but through them. As communion with God is dependent upon the broken body of Christ, so communion with one another is dependent upon realization of and participation in our universal human brokenness. O'Connor's characters who most fervently deny this brokenness, such as Asbury, Rayber, Joy/Hulga, and Sheppard, are the characters whose relationships are least whole and healthy.

A disability perspective reconstructs theology with a more horizontal soteriology. Salvation has too often been understood in vertical terms between the individual and God and has been reduced to the proclaiming of a formulaic prayer of confession, repentance, and acceptance. In this rational and autonomy-based view of salvation, the eternal destiny of persons with profound developmental disabilities, for example, is categorized under innocence, along with infants and possibly animals. The societal view of disabled people as un-whole is perpetuated, and they are not welcomed into the body of Christ as participating members with spiritual gifts to offer. In other words, even within the church Rayber's son Bishop is perceived as purposeless. A disability perspective that prioritizes relationality, however, suggests that persons with mental disabilities can be saved through relationship with their caregivers. Also, just as significantly, caregivers can be saved through their relationships with those who have mental disabilities, just as Bishop challenged his father Rayber's lack of faith. In this horizontal understanding of salvation, those whom societal norms have so often rejected from participation in religious activities are drawn into the salvific work of the body of Christ. Their spiritual gifts are employed and appreciated. They and their limitations are not mere tools used by God for a "greater" purpose. Rather, they *are* God's greater purpose. A horizontal vision of salvation, dependent upon the vulnerability required for true relationship, is much closer to the biblical witness of salvation coming through Christ's vulnerability than are the generally accepted views of salvation that rely upon autonomous rationality. Bishop being made in the image of God, then, does not only give Bishop status, but provides everyone around Bishop with a path to God.

O'Connor's example in her own life of acceptance of limitation and her insistence on the same in her stories open O'Connor's readers to the mystery of being where salvation is antithetical to modern ideals of the perfectibility of humanity. Instead she draws her readers into dependence upon God and others. The unpurposed love Bishop embodies is the height of O'Connor's theology of disability. If we are to take Bishop's humanity seriously, the *imago Dei* is better understood in terms of relationality than in terms of responsibility or dominion.[34] Because of Bishop's disability the reader is able to discern the priority relational love has over any purposeful accomplishments or purpose-driven love. The sacrament of baptism, in which all human constructions of the good are drowned before resurrected life is made possible, aptly encapsulates O'Connor's critique of modernity by pointing to human nature's original sin. The deaths of the innocent child Harry Ashfield and the developmentally disabled Bishop in these baptisms creates the greatest distance possible between the avoidance of suffering toward which modernity aspires, particularly for the innocent, and the mystery of God's activity in the world in the midst of seemingly grotesque and unnecessary suffering and even death.

Disability and the Church

O'Connor's embodied theology, shaped by her disability and the experience of her father's death, displays enormous potential for a constructive theology that aims to redefine theologies formed in the womb of modernity. More than purposing to rid the church and society of discrimination against the disabled, such a theology would require actual friendship—theologically, socially, and personally—with all forms of disability, as a realization of the relational definition of the *imago Dei*. Such a theology can work to create structures of church and society that not only make space for the disabled or appreciate them from a distance, as sentimental modern theologies have done, but that also invite the disabled to join in the ministry of the church, and, more importantly, allow the church to join in the ministries of disabled persons. O'Connor's question for her readers is profound. Can we stare at the good "long enough to accept the fact that its face too is grotesque, that in us the good is something under construction?" Or are we still too impure, unable to accept the true circumstances of our human identity?

Unfortunately, Christianity has participated in the larger society's tendency to consider persons with disabilities as persons with tragedies of limitation that need to be fixed before such persons have full communal currency. One could argue that the Enlightenment perspective has received its most complete utopian visioning in the hands of theologians and pastors who have wedded this social construction with scriptural promises of eschatological perfection and too often of a similar perfection here and now, as is the case with the health and wealth gospel and its many derivatives. The resulting view of most Christians is a belief that those with disabilities are un-whole individuals.

An example from one woman's journey with disability will be helpful. Helen Betenbaugh writes about how the church's perspective of disability affected her path to becoming a priest. Note that acceptance is central to her view and has healing properties.

> I sometimes ponder the incredible fact that I stayed in the church, that I struggled and struggled against its "truths" as I did. Segregated by lack of access, we are told by architecture and environment that we are unwanted, inferior. We are told that we have an obligation to be *cured* by the prayers of the church rather than *healed* by people's acceptance of us as we are. Ableism is a pathology, just like ageism, just like racism. We demonize those bodily states that we fear.[35]

Having taken on the socially constructed ideals of perfection, Christianity has understood healing and cure as a doing away with limitation or disease. Christianity's view of disability has therefore coincided with the Enlightenment's mandate to exterminate suffering.

Betenbaugh's long struggle to follow her calling into the priesthood was not hindered by her own disability as much as by the social factors, architecture, and attitudes that told her she was unwanted and inferior. These social determinates came to her most forcefully in letters of rejection from the bishops to whom she applied to the priesthood, letters in which she and her wheelchair were labeled "unemployable."[36] Just as O'Connor challenged the Enlightenment's utopian visioning and a disability perspective has to challenge the medical definition of normalcy, the first step for a theology of disability is to challenge the theological assumptions based on many of the same social ideals. Such a challenge can be no simple task.[37]

Anyone living in the United States today breathes in the ideal of a perfect, self-sufficient body, whether or not that person is able-bodied. Disabled persons thus often internalize the cult of normalcy and use it to measure self-worth. Betenbaugh writes about when she first felt called to be a priest: "It seemed perverse to me. The priest is an icon of Christ—of wholeness, of all that is good and right and 'perfect.' Certainly there was no place for such visible brokenness, such visible 'failure' as mine, in the priesthood of the church." As she painfully struggled with the dissonance between her body and the "perfect" body ideal of Christ, she slowly came to realize a new perspective. "I came to see that the symbol I would present would be that of an Easter life, an Easter faith, being lived in a Good Friday body. To me, then and now, that is a positive sign, an authentic sign, a holy sign. I am bold enough to say that it more clearly reflects the truth of most people's lives than a 'perfect' body does."[38] Betenbaugh is right to suggest we all live closer to a Good Friday body than a perfect body, and she is also right to note that this is a bold statement. Her acceptance of her disability flatly contradicts our culture's mythologies and ideals. O'Connor would have liked her. Betenbaugh's self-identification with a Good Friday body names ableism as the actual disability, a pathology like ageism or racism.

A realization of our Good Friday bodies is one of the most significant insights disability offers theology. Persons with disabilities are not just physical examples that help the able-bodied remember we are all broken on the inside. Rather, persons with disabilities live with an embodied vulnerability that is essential to being human,[39] an aspect of humanity the Enlightenment has denied. When disability gets used as a mere theological example, disability and vulnerability become a means to a "stronger" end. What is being suggested here is something quite different—vulnerability as the goal.[40] Theology needs disability in a similar way to how the church needs fasting. As fasting is an embodied reminder that we are more dependent upon God than even food, disability is an embodied reminder of our vulnerability in and dependence upon community. And as anyone that has practiced the discipline of fasting knows, fasting goes beyond a mere reminder. Fasting is a living into the true reality of our condition as dependent human beings.

The Practice of Disability

The theological significance of disability, and of O'Connor's life and works, is the practice of living into limitation, which involves accepting the consequences of limitation for one's life and allowing one's limitations to bring an end to one's own power. The essence of this practice is as simple as forms of meditation that empty the mind of distractions in order to allow greater focus on what is most important. The practice is also as deep, mysterious, and significant as Christ, "who, though he was in the form of God, did not regard equality with God as something to be exploited, but *emptied* himself, taking the form of a slave, being born in human likeness. And being found in human form, he humbled himself and became obedient to the point of death—even death on a cross."[41] Because the practice of disability is so antithetical to modern ways of conceiving the world, I will flesh out its meaning from three different angles before returning specifically to O'Connor's own practice of disability. We will first consider one biblical example of disability/weakness. Secondly, we will look at a dance troupe that engages and challenges our shared cultural imagination concerning disability. Lastly, we will note a case study in the practice of disability found in the L'Arche communities.

Biblical

There are, of course, very many biblical examples of weakness. The purpose here, though, is not to recount all of the stories like that of Gilead or Sarai's barrenness. Rather, I will focus on one example that highlights the biblical call to weakness as well as our modern misinterpretation (and mistranslation) of that call. In her book *Powers, Weakness and the Tabernacling of God*, Marva Dawn argues that weakness diminishes our own power, thus creating a space in which God can dwell, or tabernacle, inside us. One of her arguments, concerning 2 Corinthians 12:9, is very insightful and particularly helpful in explaining the need for weakness.

In the beginning of 2 Corinthians 12, after giving reasons why he more than anyone should be able to boast in being an apostle, Paul writes that God gave him a thorn in his side in order to keep him from "being conceited." In the NIV, 12:9 reads, "But he said to me, 'My grace is sufficient for you, for my power is made perfect in weakness.' Therefore I will boast all the more gladly about my weaknesses, so that Christ's power may rest on me." Dawn points out that the word "perfect" in the verse is translated from the Greek *teleo*, which comes from the more familiar base word *telos*, meaning end. The sense of *telos* can be understood in two different ways. First, one can speak of the end of a thing, that it is stopped or finished. Secondly, one can speak of the end as the fulfillment of a thing, that it is completed or perfected. A word study reveals that when authors in the New Testament want to express that a thing has been stopped, they use the verb *teleo*, and when they want to express that a thing has been perfected, they use the verb *teleioo*. Though *teleo* is used in 2 Corinthians 12:9, translators have consistently translated the verb as "perfected," the sense of *teleioo*. The difference between the two words and their meanings is subtle, but very meaningful. There is good reason translators have not translated *teleo* as end, like Dawn suggests. Such a translation renders the following: "My grace is sufficient for you, for my power is brought to an end in weakness." To suggest that Christ's power has been brought to an end does not fit with the context of Paul's argument.

Dawn continues her argument, though, noting that the Greek phrase for "power" in this verse lacks a pronoun. The Greek is *he dunamis*, or "the power," and can as easily be translated "your power" as "my power." If the verse is translated as referencing Paul's power, rather than Christ's, an enormous change occurs. In Dawn's translation, Christ speaks to Paul in reference to Paul's thorn and says that Paul's power is brought to an end by the thorn. The difference in the two translations is powerful: "My grace is sufficient for you, for *your* power is *brought to an end* in weakness" (Dawn) is quite dissimilar from "My grace is sufficient for you, for my power is made perfect in weakness" (NIV).

In the NIV rendering, Paul's power is a good thing, and God comes alongside Paul to help where Paul is weak. This translation fits well with our Enlightenment understandings in which we believe strongly in our own human abilities but understand that we occasionally need a little godly nudge in the right direction. In Dawn's translation, though, Paul's own power is something that must be challenged, subdued, and brought to an end, which fits better with the immediately preceding verses in which Paul references the thorn in his side that God has given him. The purpose of the thorn is to break down Paul's conceit, to keep him from boasting in his own ability. Paul's pride, the power of his will, is in contention with God's power in Paul's life. Once weakness has done its work, however, and Paul's power has been brought to an end, space is made in Paul's life for God's power:

"Therefore I will boast all the more gladly about my weaknesses, so that Christ's power may rest on me."

For Dawn, and for O'Connor, God is not interested in simply pitying our weaknesses and helping us in those places where we are not as strong as we would like. Such pitying is the very attitude from which O'Connor fled when caught on the elevator with the old lady at Davison's. Instead, O'Connor's God demands the type of submission that is willing to be drowned for the sake of baptism. Sometimes such vulnerability and weakness is created suddenly and violently, as happens in many of O'Connor's short stories, and sometimes such weakness is created through a very slow process, as happens for Rayber in *The Violent Bear It Away* and in O'Connor's struggle with lupus.

The physicality of weakness is significant here. Paul's thorn, whatever it may have been, was something physical with which he had to struggle on a daily basis. As wise and inspired as Paul was, the wisdom of weakness could not be understood through his rational learning or even a direct word from God. Weakness had to be developed by being lived. The mystery of how weakness brings our strengths to an end so that God can tabernacle within us (as Dawn puts it) cannot be told but can only be shown, and such an inhabiting of weakness is the very mystery O'Connor's fiction offers its readers.

In arguing for weakness, though, one must be careful because disability-as-symbol easily turns into sentimentality. The easy way out is to believe that we have so much we can learn from the disabled because their struggle gives them special status, special wisdom. We pity Paul that he had to deal with a thorn in his side, and we think we should pity and care for the weak because we believe God pities and cares for them. God, though, does not pity the weak. God became weak; God became disabled. As long as the able-bodied view the disabled as different from themselves—as long as anyone views an ideal body as the standard—we will continue to pity (and eliminate) the imperfect, rather than living into our shared human reality. Disability-as-symbol is only helpful insofar as it encourages us to take ownership of all our limitations, not simply those labeled "disabled." Only when we are able to realize (not philosophically understand but physically make real) our limitations will we be able to be vulnerable with one another and truly love.

Physical thorns in the flesh, though, are not the only ways of realizing weakness. The ancient Christian discipline of confession, for example, can realize mental, emotional, and spiritual weaknesses. Words can give physicality to internal weaknesses. Once spoken, such vulnerability allows the possibility for the greatest human virtues to respond: grace, forgiveness, and the kind of compassion that O'Connor says "suffers with." Unfortunately, a culture that prioritizes self-sufficiency and demonizes imperfection tends to disallow vulnerability, whether physical or emotional limitation. In doing so, our culture also denies the possibility for these virtues. O'Connor's statement is again applicable: "Busy cutting down human imperfection, they are making headway also on the raw material of good."

Cultural Imagination

The 1990 Americans with Disabilities Act (ADA) was a landmark result for the political challenge of inclusion for the disabled, and continued efforts to raise awareness since the ADA have been equally significant. These victories have altered the way people and businesses think about the disabled, from providing rights to jobs to supplying preferred parking. Unfortunately, however, our cultural imagination concerning the disabled remains stifled. Our visions of beauty, perfection, efficiency, and success continue to trade on the currency of ability and continue to marginalize those missing certain abilities.

An example from the arts helps clarify how the practice of disability can transform our cultural imaginations. The dance troupe GIMP brings this aesthetic challenge of disability to center stage. In their productions, disabled dancers are paired with able-bodied dancers—not so the able-bodied can assist the disabled, but so the unique beauty and talents of each can be explored. The director of the GIMP project, Heidi Latsky, explains,

> People go to dance events to see what they cannot do themselves. Dancers are often seen as limitless. Disabled persons are often seen as basically unable. Bringing these two groups together in GIMP questions normal ideas of dance, performance, and body image. GIMP's special mix of arms and legs offers an uncommon beauty. It examines the ways we are often identified or defined by our bodies.[42]

GIMP makes the bold assertion that beauty is not dependent on its proximity to an ideal, but beauty can instead be uncommon and abnormal. GIMP also questions the emphasis our culture puts on a certain type of body it considers normal, judging the entirety of a person according to what the eye perceives. A disability perspective critiques the ways our cultural imagination has defined us by our bodies' likeness to a constructed ideal perfection, and it reveals and promotes uncommon beauty wherever it is found. The goal is to change social/relational perceptions of persons with disabilities.

Another example from GIMP is helpful:

> GIMP is about beauty, not the photo-shopped, airbrushed kind, but a harsher more unexpected one that comes from the ultimate sexiness of risk-taking and utter commitment. . . . In GIMP, both audience and performers are aware of being watched. That provocative exchange in which our gaze is being reflected both ways leads to a shift, a questioning, and a deep sense that the frame/lens through which we view the world has somewhat changed.[43]

Creating this changed frame/lens is equally as significant as acquiring access for disabled persons, because the new perspective has the ability to transform bigotry into appreciation and transform lives destroyed by bigotry into lives appreciated in friendship. The medical (and modern) lens measures disability in its distance from normal ability, seeking to remove obstacles to normality. A disability lens allows disabled persons a space to be (political reality) as well as the possibility of being known (social reality). The new lens allows persons with disability to be beautiful, not in relation to an abstract ideal, but ontologically beautiful. The new lens also allows disabled persons to be known as unable, not in relation to an abstract "normal" ability but in relation to self and in relation to the reality of universal limitation. Unfortunately the vast majority of us hide our weaknesses, not wanting them to be known, and we thus miss out on the opportunity to be fully known.

The significance of a disability perspective lies in its capacity to probe and critique our assumptions about what is normal and purposefully to include within our cultural makeup the insights, creativity, and strengths disabled persons contribute. Perhaps a way forward in countering the demonizing of weakness could be to associate our weaknesses with beauty, as GIMP has done. O'Connor's work is consistently significant in both critiquing our culture and contributing a new vision. Her stories powerfully call into question what we define as normal and good, and her stories' insights and true beauty lie precisely in those places we find abnormal or grotesque.

L'Arche

Perhaps the best example to clarify the practice of limitation can be found in a group of communities around the world that have lived the truth of disability for nearly fifty years. The first L'Arche community began in 1964 in France, when Jean Vanier decided to share his life with three developmentally disabled men. There are now over 140 L'Arche communities in 36 countries. In their homes, people with and without intellectual disabilities live together in community with the purpose of realizing the unique gifts of each individual. A research project in the UK explored the spiritual lives of persons with developmental disabilities and their caregivers. One of the primary groups the project studied was L'Arche communities.[44]

The first thing researchers noted is that as their team spent time with caregivers and support workers, they were struck by "the way in which people's lives and worldviews have been radically transformed through their encounters with people who have profound developmental disabilities. [Their] lives are changed, their priorities are reshaped and their vision of God and humanness are altered at their very core." They named this change "a process of *transvaluation* within which personal encounter with people with profound developmental

disabilities initiates a movement towards a radically new system
of valuing."[45]

The process of transvaluation involves learning to love and
to be loved, and it embraces vulnerability as the locus of a life
that realizes, or makes real, relationships of love. In contrast to
Enlightenment understandings that seek to fix the "problems"
of developmental disabilities or to manage the problems found
unfixable or to provide the prenatal testing that would make
these problems disappear altogether, transvaluation results in a
deep valuing of those with developmental disabilities. In contrast as well to a liberatory theology, whose goal is to fix the
situation of the poor, Swinton argues,

> God is with the poor, not in triumphalistic revolution, but in the
> weakness and vulnerability that is experienced in the everyday tasks
> of living together in community. . . . The experiences of people with
> profound developmental disabilities remind us of dimensions of God
> which have been hidden by our culture's preference for such things as
> power, strength and intellectual prowess.[46]

Cultural ideals and theologies that focus on the triumph of
individuals have created a fear of limitation and suffering. Culture has stigmatized those with visible deficiencies as deviants,
because they embody our fears of failure and death. However,
"The communal life of L'Arche and its daily encounters with the
weak, the poor and the voiceless, and its ability to see God in the
midst of these encounters, moves us away from idolization and
the flight from suffering, and forces us to consider the possibility
that the nature, character and actions of God may be radically
different from our socially constructed norms."[47] Rather than
liberation being an extraction from circumstances that are painful and broken, at L'Arche "liberation comes when people begin
to let go of their individuality and to recognize the strength that
comes from gentleness, mutuality, weakness and brokenness. In
this way, those who accompany people in L'Arche find themselves, who they are, what they are, why they are, in the mutuality of life with others."[48] The assistants "begin to reconstruct who

they are as persons-in-relation both with God and with other human beings."[49]

At L'Arche, they find a lived experience of a theology of disability that takes seriously the limitations of the incarnation and the disabilities of the cross. The disabled find a community that embodies the mystery Paul speaks of in 1 Corinthians that "God chose the foolish things of the world to shame the wise; God chose the weak things of the world to shame the strong. He chose the lowly things of this world and the despised things" (1 Cor 1:27-28). In fact, God chose the cross, which Paul names in a single verse as "foolishness" to this world and yet "the power of God" (1 Cor 1:20). At L'Arche they find that the things our societal standards have labeled as weak, foolish, and disposable actually hold within them the true power of living and loving. Those who are willing to be vulnerable, to be needed as well as to need, experience the freedom of non-autonomy and the liveliness of communal sufficiency.

O'Connor's Practice of Disability

During her writing career, O'Connor awoke each day with pain. Her bed was moved to the first floor in the living area so she would not have to traverse the stairs. As she prepared to go to mass, she moved from room to room using crutches. Some years she had to be careful to be completely covered before going outside, so her lupus would not be inflamed by the sunlight. Attending mass was its own limitation. Theologically, it was a reminder of God's limitation in the incarnation and the cross. Also, though, attending mass used a good portion of the scarce energy she had for a day. Once she returned, she could do little else besides write, and that only for the remainder of the morning. Her habit of being was a habit of limitation, both chosen and not chosen, a habit she understood as a gateway to reality.

In the preceding examples, particularly in L'Arche, we see how disability and limitation allow access to our true reality as humans. That access, though, does not occur through reason alone, because insight into our true humanity does not happen through understanding *that* we are limited. Rather, our true reality is revealed as we practice the grace, forgiveness, and love that limitation allows. Limitation is only the gateway, the first step, and O'Connor's fiction shouts this truth past our Enlightened deafness to it. Though our society has come to appreciate some limitation, we have not comprehended the full limitation of disability. Our culture appreciates limitation as a "problem to be solved," as Rayber puts it. For the Enlightened, limitation is a scientific conundrum and is useful only in its ability to help us come up with creative solutions. Whatever does not kill us, as the saying goes, makes us stronger. The evolutionary objective is to be stronger. However, disability (particularly developmental disability) calls our culture's view of limitation into question. Often, disabilities cannot be overcome, as O'Connor's lupus could not be. For another example, there can be no "stronger" Bishop. Even theologically, there can be no Enlightened justification for Bishop's existence. As long as we attempt to deny limitation, ultimately denying death, Bishop will remain other to us, distant and unwanted. When we realize our common vulnerability, though, we will accept him as one of us, and we may learn to accept the reality of our own vulnerability and need for salvation.

There is hardly an area of O'Connor's life that was not affected by her lupus and was thus not limited. However, unlike Asbury in "The Enduring Chill," O'Connor embraced her limitations. Asbury could not acknowledge any part of his life—the return to his rural town or even his own writing. His limitations became for him a gateway to death, at least until he was forced to recognize his limitations as his own and not his mother's or his culture's or God's. In the throes of accepting his own limitations is where the possibility of the descent of the Holy Ghost occurs, the mysterious work of God that creates life and possibility out of death and limitation. After acknowledging his own limitation he might recognize and appreciate his mother's grace and love for him. But as O'Connor was fond of saying, that is another story. Perhaps it was O'Connor's story.

A Disability Perspective for O'Connor Studies

There can be little doubt that O'Connor's own struggle with lupus greatly contributed to her appreciation of limitation, an appreciation I contend is essential to understanding her work. O'Connor scholarship, though, has dealt very little with O'Connor's disability, and when it has done so, it has sometimes gravely missed the point. In an article entitled "Coping with Lupus," for example, Gretchen Dobrott relates O'Connor's disability to her writing. She writes that O'Connor "felt that the physical diminishment brought on by lupus enhanced her literature, and she apparently accepted this exchange as a reasonable price to pay for her talent. By perceiving disability and death as significant elements of her own spiritual development, acceptance became much easier."[50] Certainly O'Connor accepted her illness as part of God's plan, but she surely would have cringed at accepting it "as a reasonable price to pay." Disability as a reasonable price to pay suggests a God who barters, giving this-much-suffering for the sake of this-much-talent. Disability as a reasonable price to pay is Asbury's perception of his illness in "The Enduring Chill," a view O'Connor obviously critiques in the story. In addition to being a conception of God with which O'Connor would have strongly disagreed, Dobrott's suggestion is dependent on the Enlightenment concern for ability-as-identity that O'Connor ultimately critiques.

Dobrott's misconception reveals itself in her critiques of O'Connor's stories. She writes,

> The sexual undertones of "Good Country People" and the numerous coincidences between its protagonist and the author encourage one to seriously consider the possibility that the sordid love scene in the barn and its resolution were not only devised to initiate a redeeming experience but to also, perhaps unintentionally, unleash her feelings about her lack of self-sufficiency, the physical limitations brought on by her illness, the side-effects of the large doses of cortisone that she was given, and the social constraints of a small town in rural, fervently Protestant Georgia.[51]

I comment on Dobrott's argument for two reasons. First, I believe Dobrott is overreaching. She gives very little evidence for her argument except showing that O'Connor was not self-sufficient. Secondly, and more importantly, Dobrott's argument provides an excellent example of why a disability-studies perspective is needed in literary criticism and more specifically in O'Connor studies. Dobrott's critique here assumes O'Connor expected self-sufficiency and unlimited physicality as a sort of human right, which is closer to the opposite of how O'Connor viewed self-sufficiency. Dobrott begins with the modern Western assumptions about what it means to be human and what is important in life—mobility and pristine health allowing for the greatest autonomy—and presumes O'Connor felt "crippled" in relation to these ideals. A disability-studies perspective on O'Connor, however, drastically changes the interpretation of this story.[52]

Far from being a conscious or subconscious emergence of her disgust with her disability's effect on her life, the story's tension and grotesque ending serve as a critique of a social system that requires self-sufficiency and autonomy. O'Connor's story critiques the American liberalism that has taken hold in Joy/Hulga and that is presumed in Dobrott's analysis of O'Connor. Joy/Hulga had taken on the modern assumptions concerning self-sufficiency and reason as the primary goals of life, and the loss of the artificial leg at the end of the story robs her of this wooden part of her soul. Once relieved of her illusion of self-sufficiency, she is made ready for the possibility of grace, though portraying such grace was admittedly not O'Connor's unique talent.

My counterargument to Dobrott would not hold water if evidence existed in O'Connor's letters or any other writings that suggested she was frustrated and angry about her disability's effect on her life. About as frustrated as she got was at the very end of her life when she admitted to being "sick of being sick."[53] She never, however, expressed a larger philosophical or theological angst toward her illness. In fact, those who knew her were surprised at how little she complained about her pain, much less her situation.[54] My argument would also be weak if there were no indication at all, whether positive or negative, about how she viewed her disability. Perhaps then we could suppose a subconscious upheaval of the grotesque, as Dobrott suggests. However, when one considers O'Connor's other writings, it is undeniable that she understood her disability very differently from Dobrott's suggestion.

O'Connor's cousin Katie Semmes once insisted that Flannery and her mother go to Lourdes in France, so Flannery could find healing at the pools there. With her typical wit, O'Connor described the trip to Elizabeth Bishop in a letter in 1958, noting that "They passed around a thermos bottle of Lourdes water and everybody had to take a drink out of the top. I had a nasty cold so I figured I left more germs than I took away." She then writes of the "medieval hygiene" of the pools and says, "I saw nothing but peasants and was very conscious of the distinct odor of the crowd. The supernatural is a fact there but it displaces nothing natural; except maybe those germs."[55] In another letter she confessed, "I prayed there for the novel I was working on, not for my bones which I care about less."[56] The suffering lupus caused her was not something she actively sought deliverance from, not even through any mysterious spiritual means that proffered themselves to her. Rather, the lupus was a diminishment she fully accepted, an acceptance that runs counter to any definition of being human that has its foundation in ability.

Dobrott's argument assumes O'Connor's feelings toward lupus from an outside perspective. Though she is well-intentioned, she participates in what O'Connor would consider mere sentimentality. Dobrott assumes the deviance from normality that is in O'Connor's story reflects O'Connor's own deviation from the normality of a self-sufficient life. O'Connor is, of course, deviating from normality, but not as a subconscious unleashing of "her feelings about her lack of self-sufficiency." Rather, she is critiquing the normalcy of self-sufficiency and autonomy.[57]

Dobrott makes the same mistake reviewers of O'Connor's first collection of short stories made. Lamenting the fact that reviewers of her book misunderstood her, remember that

O'Connor wrote, "The stories are hard but they are hard because there is nothing harder or less sentimental than Christian realism. . . . When I see these stories described as horror stories I am always amused because the reviewer always has hold of the wrong horror."[58] O'Connor's actual deviance from the normal is a deviance from what she considered the demonic modern assumption of self-sufficiency as foundational to being human, an assumption in which Dobrott's analysis participates.

O'Connor's feelings about her disability are likely much more in line with Peter Huggins' poem entitled "Flannery O'Connor at Lourdes," which begins:

> Mother's idea to bring me here.
> I could care less about a cure.
> I know what God intends for me.
> Why should I postpone the inevitable?
> It makes no sense: I have accepted
> My fate. Why can't Mother?[59]

Rather than taking out her frustrations concerning the lack of self-sufficiency her disability caused, she saw her disability "with the blind, prophetical, unsentimental eye of acceptance."[60] Such acceptance is an act of faith that places one's life within the confines of a world that God, and not humanity, controls.

Complications of Language and Representation

Despite the heavy influence of disability studies upon this book, I have attempted to keep the main text of the book free of disability-studies language and academic arguments. My goal has been to reimagine O'Connor's work from a disability perspective and thereby to offer a new interpretation of her significance. The danger of my method lies in being misunderstood, and one concern in particular may have left readers with some discomfort, especially those familiar with disability studies. The correct use of language concerning disability is complex and continuously evolving, and the literary use of disability as a metaphor is even more complicated. The purpose of this postscript is to uncover the complexity of the issues involved as well as to provide some explanation for why I at times used the terms *disability* and *grotesque* interchangeably.

Disability studies tends to critique any use of disability-as-metaphor, which O'Connor uses regularly in her work. The problem disability studies has with authors using disability-as-metaphor is related to how our culture perceives disability negatively. Representations of disability in literature are nearly always negative metaphors, which only serve to reinforce negative stereotypes.

The point I want to make concerning O'Connor's use of disability-as-metaphor is not that O'Connor's representations of disability are above reproach. Sometimes O'Connor does use disability as little more than a metaphor to propel forward the action and meaning of a story, and these instances require a strong critique. A disability perspective is right to suggest that the use of disability-as-metaphor reinforces the cultural tendency to totalize persons with disabilities and assign some negative meaning to their condition. However, to lump together all of O'Connor's uses of the disabled and grotesque as merely metaphorical or just a literary tool fails to observe the larger categories of meaning O'Connor employs as well as the development of her technical use of the grotesque. To put it differently, O'Connor's use of disability is not so simplistic as equating disability with the aesthetic category of the grotesque, at least not solely in a negative sense.

In light of the above, I proceeded cautiously and with a certain dialectic as I explored the complex relationship between disability and the grotesque in O'Connor's fiction. I sought to affirm a disability critique of the reductive, aesthetic use of disability-as-metaphor while acknowledging the necessity and possible benefits of a new vision of disability-as-metaphor in O'Connor's writings. What makes O'Connor's employment of disability so complex is the tension between her regular use of disability as a negative metaphor and the fact that the larger concepts and intentions behind O'Connor's use of disability are often aligned with the values and aims of disability studies. Adding to the complexity, O'Connor so thoroughly refutes modernity that she implicates even disability studies in the process. Instead of using the grotesque and disabilities only as metaphor, O'Connor comes to use the grotesque to challenge modern social perceptions of what is good and bad, to embody the necessity of accepting limitations, and to create an example of how what we consider grotesque can be a conduit for God's grace in the world.

From a disability perspective, O'Connor's employment of the grotesque is problematic because the grotesque runs the risk of turning her characters into mere caricatures. Many of her earliest readers viewed her stories as mere embodiments of caricatures, with Northern literary critics laughing at the bumbling idiots in the South. Of course O'Connor's Southern family and fellow Milledgevillians were afraid of becoming the objects of ridicule. At first glance, O'Connor's caricatures perpetuate harmful stereotypes of the South—of race, of conservative Christians, and of the physically and mentally disabled.

As disability studies has begun to engage literary studies, its primary concern has been with the way disability is represented in literature. Authors of fiction include disability, as with every other detail, for a specific purpose, and disability generally gets used as a negative metaphor.[1] O'Connor's representations of the disabled are no exception.[2] O'Connor's and her critics' discussion of human variation in her fiction, therefore, has largely used the aesthetic language of the "grotesque," even when discussing the disabled. Grotesque is a term a disability perspective does not take lightly. Considering only the aesthetic utility of race and gender, especially in terms of the grotesque, while ignoring the political realities of race and gender would be unthinkable for readers. A disability perspective argues that critiquing disability only in aesthetic terms should likewise be unthinkable. Yet aesthetic-only readings of disability in O'Connor's fiction abound.

Disabled bodies and minds in O'Connor's fiction are viewed as part of her participation in the school of the Southern grotesque, a group of authors loosely tied together by their regional writing who create "grotesque" characters and actions. In the school, grotesqueries are physical metaphors for social ills that the authors are attempting to unmask. A disability critique is uncomfortable with disabled characters being subsumed under the categorization of the grotesque and not being dealt with as individuals.[3] Readings of O'Connor have taken these representations-as-metaphors for granted, both because the larger field of literature studies has done so and because O'Connor herself did so. Even the title of O'Connor's essay "Some Aspects of the Grotesque in Southern Fiction" shows how deeply influenced she was by the school of the Southern grotesque.

A disability perspective critiques the use of disability as a representation for social ills for two primary reasons. First, such representation continues to propagate a perceived link between disability and deviance.[4] Disability continues to operate in most of society's imagination as the negative "other," the embodiment of what one hopes not to become. Of course, the grotesque in O'Connor's fiction always works metaphorically. One need only reference her famous quote that "you have to make your vision apparent by shock—to the hard of hearing you shout, and for the almost blind you draw large and startling figures."[5] She puts a similar sentiment in a letter, stating, "I am interested in making up a good case for distortion, as I am coming to believe it is the only way to make people see."[6] Since modern culture cannot hear and see its grotesque *interior*, O'Connor paints the grotesque on her characters' *exterior* actions and bodies. The difficulty from a disability perspective is in the tying together of moral evil and physical disfigurement. Her disabled and grotesque characters become the distorted shouts and startling figures required to shock her readers that are "hard of hearing" her message and "almost blind" to her prophetic vision. Disability therefore often functions in her stories in precisely this negative way, as a representation of sin and evil. At least, negative representation is her early view of the grotesque's function in her work.

The other primary problem with disability as representation is that when disability gets reduced to a function in the story, the person with the disability becomes no more than an embodiment of the loss that the story attempts to communicate, and the lived reality of the character with the disability gets ignored. In other words, the disabled become mere tools. The result is a reinforcing of the totalizing effect disability already has in our society, an effect that displaces the whole of the person in favor of fascination with or repulsion from the disability itself. The fullness of being a human is ignored, and real people are reduced to one aspect of their lives.

As with race and gender studies, then, a disability perspective insists upon a sociopolitical reading.[7] However, avoiding the aesthetic-only readings of O'Connor is difficult, in part because O'Connor was largely unconcerned with the sociopolitical realities of her characters.[8] Her primary concern was spiritual, and she uses whatever means available to do her shouting. Her style therefore allows and even perpetuates negative stereotypes of disability.

For example, in "The Life You Save May Be Your Own," Lucynell Carter is deaf and dumb. Her mother, in an attempt to sell her to a suitor, tells Mr. Shiftlet, "One who can't talk . . . can't sass you back or use foul language. That's the kind for you to have. Right there." Shiftlet replies, "That's right . . . She wouldn't give me any trouble."[9] The complexity of who Lucynell is, her talents, gifts, or anything she could offer to the relationship, is ignored, except of course for her ability to "sweep the floor, cook, wash, feed the chickens, and hoe,"[10] which her mother describes earlier in the story. Shiftlet and Lucynell's mother choose Lucynell's life for her without consulting her or being concerned in the least with what she desires. All of the above are red flags for a disability reading. O'Connor's use of disability in "The Life You Save May Be Your Own" has problematic elements that must be addressed, and the question of whether or not O'Connor uses disability in some stories purely aesthetically is hardly up for debate and needs to be critiqued.

However, though a disability perspective can take some cues from race and gender readings, ultimately disability is different. Disability is fluid, happening to different persons at different stages of life and having both negative and positive aspects. Also, unlike readings concerned with race or gender, disability cannot claim a *lack* of representation in literature. Rather, disability may well be overrepresented in literature.[11] The problem, again, is that persons with disabilities are often used as metaphors for some other lack within the story, whether it be a character's moral makeup or a country's military impotence. The *person* becomes a mere embodiment of the useful metaphor that is her disability, and her internal experiences are left unexplored.

O'Connor explains her story "Good Country People" along the lines of metaphorical utility. She notes that Joy/Hulga's wooden leg accumulates meaning throughout the story, setting up the story's revelation: "She believes in nothing but her own belief in nothing, and we perceive that there is a wooden part of her soul that corresponds to the wooden leg."[12] In another essay she writes that "it is when the freak can be sensed as a figure for our essential displacement that he attains some depth in literature."[13] These quotes evidence her understanding of the aesthetic and metaphorical utility of the lame and the freaks in her stories.

Yet disability-as-metaphor in literature is inevitable, because disability is very useful as a metaphor. In their book *Narrative Prosthesis*, Mitchell and Snyder argue this utility is not necessarily problematic. They suggest disability acts as a prosthetic limb to literature. It is an appendage that is functional, even necessary, but always unnaturally attached and uncomfortable. Everything in a story is put there for a reason, and a disability is no different. The purpose for inserting disability is usually to contrast the normal with what is different, thus demarcating the boundary line between the self and the "other." Consequently, the normative actually depends on the abnormal for its very existence. Authors of fiction are then able to use the distance created between the normal and the abnormal for emotional effect and implicit meaning. The question that disability-influenced literature studies must ask, then, is, what are the implicit meanings?

In addition to being inevitable, disability-as-metaphor is necessary. There is little in literature that is not used metaphorically. As a disability perspective approaches literature, then, it must do two things. First it must acknowledge and critique the many uses of disability that, while not fully illegitimate, often reinforce poor cultural perspectives of disability—both that a disabled person is little more than the disability and that a disabled person is not normal and needs to be fixed, just as Hulga's wooden soul obviously needs to be fixed. Along the same lines, a disability perspective must encourage fictional explorations of the disabled that represent them as whole people.

Secondly, and with great care, disability and literature studies cannot dismiss aesthetic uses of disability out of hand, but must instead consider the author's metaphorical meaning. In O'Connor's case, these metaphors are often challenging the very cultural assumptions that wield power over the disabled. Continuing the previous example, the disability that makes Lucynell Carter a "good wife" because she cannot sass Mr. Shiftlet can be interpreted in multiple ways. One way is to see that O'Connor is providing a negative example of how the disabled should be treated. In doing so, she shocks the reader with how this young woman is treated while holding Lucynell up as the sole positive character in the story. Though the reader sees her disability as a negative metaphor, the reader also perceives that society's negative understanding of Lucynell is undeserved. Another interpretation would suggest the other characters' consideration of Lucynell as a "good wife" because she cannot sass is O'Connor's ironic critique of the cultural mores of a subservient wife whose primary use is hoeing.[14] Thus, O'Connor uses the negative stereotypes against Lucynell to critique larger social categories that reach beyond disability but would ultimately include Lucynell's disability as well.

A similar understanding can be brought to many of O'Connor's negative uses of disability. Most powerful, in my opinion, is her use of Bishop in *The Violent Bear It Away*, as I have already noted. One more example, though, will further clarify my point. In "Good Country People," Joy/Hulga's wooden leg is certainly used as a negative example of the wooden part of her soul. The wooden part of her soul is her reliance upon reason alone and the absence of any ability to accept her wooden leg and her lot in life. She stomps around as a disembodied head, attempting to be fully independent and in need of no one. O'Connor's larger critique, though, is against a modern, reason-only society that has little need for a body or a soul or a community. Though O'Connor uses this disability as a negative metaphor, the metaphor aligns with disability studies' emphases on embodiment, acceptance, and community.

Examining disability-as-representation must be carefully attentive to sociopolitical concerns while not disregarding the power and necessity of metaphor within literature. O'Connor lived before the time of political correctness and would likely have been little concerned with political correctness even if she were alive today. Her characters regularly espouse harmful views of disability, and she consistently uses disability as a metaphor for original sin, not always paying attention to the lived reality of the disabled. From a particular disability perspective, there is much to critique and dismiss. However, when one takes seriously the power and purpose of metaphor, O'Connor must be reconsidered, particularly in light of her other discussions about limitation and acceptance.

I chose to reference disability and the grotesque interchangeably for reasons similar to O'Connor reasons for using disability-as-metaphor. My larger theological concern in this book has been to suggest a theology of limits that includes us all. We are *all* grotesque, and our grotesqueries and limitations are our gateways to reality. In my writing, I attempted to make this shift fully, not to view the grotesque as only negative. From this particular perspective, then, relating disability to the grotesque is not problematic; rather, it is a view of disability that does not perceive disability negatively.

Notes

Chapter One

1   Flannery O'Connor, *The Habit of Being* (New York: Farrar, Straus & Giroux, 1980), 163 (hereafter cited as *HB*).

2   Just as her doing what she had "done in Milledgeville" would have been to the Romans. In a letter to Maryat Lee on May 19, 1957, O'Connor wrote, "My standard is: when in Rome, do as you done in Milledgeville." *HB*, 220.

3   Flannery O'Connor, *The Complete Stories of Flannery O'Connor* (New York: Noonday, 1971), 133 (hereafter cited as *CS*).

4   *HB*, 442.

5   Flannery O'Connor, *Mystery and Manners* (New York: Farrar, Straus & Giroux, 1957), 215 (hereafter cited as *M&M*).

6   *M&M*, 225.

7   *M&M*, 226.

8   *M&M*, 209.

9   *HB*, 234.

10 You can watch the video at British Pathé Online, accessed August 16, 2011, http://www.britishpathe.com/record.php?id=28819. The backwards-walking chicken is a point Brad Gooch makes a great deal about in his recent biography of O'Connor. He centers his prologue on this story, naming the prologue "Walking Backward"; see Gooch, *Flannery: A Life of Flannery O'Connor* (New York: Little, Brown, 2009), 3–9.

11 *M&M*, 3.
12 *M&M*, 4.
13 Gooch, *Flannery*, 242 and 224, respectively.
14 A collection of these cartoons was published in December 2011 under the title *Flannery O'Connor: The Cartoons.*
15 Gooch, *Flannery*, 77–78.
16 Christina Bieber Lake writes about being inspired by how O'Connor dealt with these limitations, noting, "O'Connor lived in a time and culture in which female intellectuals were much more maligned and misunderstood." Bieber Lake is "even more amazed by her cheerful faithfulness, her complete lack of maudlin sentimentality, and most of all, her commitment to her vocation, in spite of her failing body. This is a woman who knew about limitations." Bieber Lake, "Vocation through Limitation: Flannery O'Connor's Life of Faith," *The Cresset* 71, no. 4 (2008): 6–13, available online at http://www.thecresset.org/.
17 *M&M*, 131.
18 *M&M*, 193.
19 *M&M*, 68.
20 *M&M*, 133.
21 For more on the ethical effect of living with a disability, see Jackie Leach Scully's "Drawing Lines, Crossing Lines: Ethics and the Challenge of Disabled Embodiment," in which she argues, "the lived experience of a specific embodiment affects the structures of imagination and interpretation that people use in moral perception and evaluation." Scully, *Feminist Theology* 11, no. 3 (2003): 265.
22 *M&M*, 183.
23 O'Connor wrote, "The only thing I wrestle with is the language and a certain poverty of means in handling it, but this is merely what you have to do to write at all." *M&M*, 40.
24 Because lupus drained her energies, she had to structure her days very precisely in order to maximize her creative output. She was not able, for example, to take the morning off to go into town for shopping and then write in the afternoon, because she would be too worn out by that time to concentrate and be creative.
25 *HB*, 257.
26 Spelling in O'Connor's letters is often tongue in cheek. *HB*, 582.
27 Wendy Thomas notes, "With all this joking, one might miss the sense of suffering that she must have felt during these years. Her sentences are almost entirely devoid of the pain and violence of disease she must have endured." Thomas, "More Instructive Than a Long Trip to

Europe: The Effects of Lupus on Flannery O'Connor's Short Stories"
(Master's thesis, University of New Brunswick, 1997), 12.

28 Thomas notes that in addition to some of the more common side
effects of lupus, in her letters O'Connor also mentions the lupus causing "popping jaws (HB 397), porous bones (HB 397), sun intolerance
(MM 322), kidney failure (MM 584), anemia (HB 564), and many flus
and colds; but she seemed to be most affected by her lack of energy,
something from which she got little relief." Thomas, "More Instructive," 3, 77.

29 *HB,* 26. Jennifer Profitt notes, "ATCH is effective in reducing the
inflammation associated with lupus. However, given high doses over
the long term (as O'Connor was), ATCH produces a host of undesirable physical side effects: atrophy, Cushing syndrome, thrombo-
cytopenia (splotched skin), anemia, bone deterioration, tumors, and
insomnia—all of which O'Connor suffered." Jennifer Profitt, "Lupus
and Corticosteroid Imagery in the Works of Flannery O'Connor," *Flannery O'Connor Bulletin* 26–27 (2000): 77.

30 *HB,* 322.

31 *HB,* 380.

32 Quoted in Thomas, "More Instructive," 14.

33 Jennifer Profitt notes, "One must ask why, with the intense scholarly
interest in Flannery O'Connor's work, there has been so little written,
and with such hesitancy, about her illness as influence on her writing."
She goes on to suggest, "This absence of research into O'Connor's illness as source reflects a generalized, societal avoidance and discomfort
with the intimacies of disability." Profitt, "Lupus," 75.

34 Similarly, see *The Handbook of Disability Studies'* explanation of Leslie
Fiedler's seminal work *Pity and Fear: Myths and Images of the Disabled in Literature Old and New.* "Fiedler's (1981) argument rests on
a complication of the idea of unsatisfactory imagery by framing the
question of literary representation within a psychoanalytical framework. The ambivalence sensed by readers in literary presentations of
disabled characters is akin to a vicarious experience of culture's uncer-
tainty about their disabled populations." The fact of critics' silence
concerning O'Connor's disability proves this point all the more. David
Mitchell and Sharon Snyder, "Representation and Its Discontents: The
Uneasy Home of Disability in Literature and Film," in *The Handbook of Disability Studies,* ed. Gary Albrecht, Katherine Seelman, and
Michael Bury (Thousand Oaks, Calif.: Sage, 2001), 209.

35 Jean Cash points out, "Since O'Connor—alienated by both her
individuality and genius—had never been particularly comfortable

in Milledgeville, she, on her return, had to make compromises and adjustments that would enable her to continue to develop and use her unique talents. She had to accept the *limitations* imposed on her by lupus erythematosus, restrictions that partly influenced her writing schedule and certainly controlled her travel away from Milledgeville." Cash, *Flannery O'Connor: A Life* (Knoxville: University of Tennessee Press, 2002), 134; emphasis added.

36 *HB*, 224.
37 *HB*, 230.
38 *HB*, 285.
39 *HB*, 91.
40 *HB*, 57.
41 *HB*, 234.
42 *HB*, 590.
43 *HB*, 139.
44 Concerning *The Habit of Being*, the published collection of O'Connor's letters, Jill Baumgaertner argues the book amounts to a diary and the letters "bring into clearer focus the human being behind the art. The collection was an invaluable contribution to scholarship, and has, since its publication, offered readers information that is indispensable in understanding the author." Baumgaertner, "'The Meaning Is in You': Flannery O'Connor in Her Letters," *Christian Century* 104, no. 39 (1987): 1172.
45 Wendy Thomas writes, "For the most part, she refers little to the suffering her deteriorating condition must have inevitably caused. In many instances she appears light-hearted about it." Thomas, "More Instructive," 11.
46 *HB*, 585.
47 "O'Connor's Christian faith and the modern secular spirit—these two ingredients collided to produce her remarkable fiction." Michael M. Jordan, "Flannery O'Connor's Writing: A Guide for the Perplexed," *MA* 47, no. 1 (2005), available online at http://www.firstprinciplesjournal.com/articles.aspx?article=782&theme=homepage=1&loc=b&type=cttf.
48 *HB*, 116–17.
49 *M&M*, 146.
50 *M&M*, 148. Denise T. Askin comments helpfully on this point: "The journey toward God, O'Connor claimed, is often impeded by emotion, particularly when it leads one to skip the process of redemption 'in its concrete reality' in order to arrive at a 'mock state of innocence, which strongly suggests its opposite' (*Mystery and Manners* 148). 'A mind cleared of false emotion and false sentiment and egocentricity,' O'Connor says, 'is going to have at least those roadblocks removed

from its path' (*Mystery and Manners* 84). Her animus against emotion amounted to a virtual campaign against sentimentality and sappy compassion. She was dogged by readers who wanted to feel compassion for her cripples and idiots while she wanted 'intellectual and moral judgments . . . [to] have ascendancy over feeling' (*Mystery and Manners* 43). She levels her aim at pious readers and writers, people 'afflicted with sensibility' (*Mystery and Manners* 84), who produce and reward 'soggy, formless' literature (*Mystery and Manners* 31). In 'The Church and the Fiction Writer' she goes so far as to link sentimentality in art with obscenity and pornography (*Mystery and Manners* 147–48), both guilty of the Manichean tendency to separate nature and grace." Askin, "Anagogical Vision and Comedic Form in Flannery O'Connor: The Reasonable Use of the Unreasonable," *Renascence* 57, no. 1 (2004): 47–62.

51 See Fiedler, *Pity and Fear.*

52 Nancy Eisland notes that throughout history "disability has never been religiously neutral, but shot through with theological significance." Eisland, *The Disabled God: Toward a Liberatory Theology of Disability* (Nashville: Abingdon, 1994), 69–70.

53 Eisland, who wrote about hearing these folk theodicies as she grew up in the church, concludes her thoughts with an O'Connor-like, humorous rejection of such revelations of God's supposed purposes: "I was told God gave me a disability to develop my character. But at the age of six or seven, I was convinced that I had enough character to last a lifetime." Eisland, "Barriers and Bridges: Relating the Disability Rights Movement and Religious Organizations," in *Human Disability and the Service of God: Reassessing Religious Practice*, ed. Nancy Eisland and Don E. Saliers, 200–229 (Nashville: Abingdon, 1998).

54 Bieber Lake writes, "O'Connor read a version of intellectual history in which America's spiritual blindness was definitively linked to the Enlightenment." Christina Bieber Lake, *The Incarnational Art of Flannery O'Connor* (Macon, Ga.: Mercer University Press, 2005), 16.

55 *M&M*, 41.

56 Bieber Lake, *Incarnational Art*, 16.

57 Bieber Lake notes, "In Cartesian dualism only the mind that has been purified of all contamination by the body or the outside world could be trusted to reason its way to the truth." *Incarnational Art*, 17.

58 *HB*, 74.

59 *HB*, 302–3.

60 She writes that the notion of the perfectibility of humanity "is what the South has traditionally opposed. . . . The South in other words still

believes that man has fallen and that he is only perfectible by God's grace, not by his own unaided efforts." *HB*, 25.

61 *M&M*, 227.

62 *M&M*, 226–27.

63 The result, as Wood notes, is that our culture seeks "to cure every evil, whether mental or physical, with an appropriate therapy. The avoidance of suffering becomes the single criterion, therefore, for determining the good, and pain becomes the chief measure of evil." Ralph Wood, *Flannery O'Connor and the Christ-Haunted South* (Grand Rapids: Eerdmans, 2004), 198.

64 Wood writes, "The chief temptation of nihilism is to employ force in order to accomplish alleged good. There being no transcendent order by which human desires might be reordered to the Good, we must both devise and enforce our own schemes for human betterment." Ralph Wood, "Sacramental Suffering: The Friendship of Flannery O'Connor and Elizabeth Hester," *Modern Theology* 24, no. 3 (2008): 391.

65 *M&M*, 226.

66 Wood writes, "Because [O'Connor] learned to make her affliction into a sacramental participation in Christ's own suffering, [Mary Ann's] soul enabled her body to take its true form in a graciously embraced death. In the absence of such faith, the suffering inherent in the natural order is no longer the means of redemption. Nature is, instead, a purposeless realm awaiting human manipulation. The secular conclusion, therefore, is that Mary Ann's life is a mistake of nature and should have been aborted, since she made no contribution to society." Wood, "Sacramental Suffering," 405–6.

67 From a letter O'Connor wrote to Hester on October 31, 1956, quoted in Wood, "Sacramental Suffering," 408.

68 Flannery O'Connor, *Collected Works* (New York: Literary Classics of the United States, 1988), 823 (hereafter cited as *CW*).

69 *CW*, 823.

70 Bieber Lake writes, "In the story Alymer is a modern scientist who, under the influence of pure Cartesian categories, tries to use science to eliminate anything he considers to be impure and mysterious in human existence. . . . The little birthmark wrecks Alymer's worship of the perfectibility of humanity, of the scientific mind's ability to escape what it deems to be messy." Bieber Lake, *Incarnational Art*, 211–12.

71 *M&M*, 223.

72 As Wood points out, O'Connor attempted to help Hester understand her suffering in this light as well. Wood concludes, "The longer one peruses these letters to Betty Hester, both before and after she called

herself a Christian, the more it becomes evident that [for O'Connor] Christian faith has one requisite above all others—namely, it entails a gift of total self-surrender, an unstinting willingness to participate in the suffering of Christ for the redemption of the world." Wood, "Sacramental Suffering," 392–93.

73 *HB*, 543.
74 *M&M*, 227.

Chapter Two

1 Flannery O'Connor, *The Complete Stories of Flannery O'Connor* (New York: Noonday, 1971), 491 (hereafter cited as *CS*).
2 *CS*, 497.
3 *CS*, 491.
4 *CS*, 491.
5 *CS*, 488.
6 *CS*, 489.
7 *CS*, 490.
8 *CS*, 495.
9 Flannery O'Connor, *Mystery and Manners* (New York: Farrar, Straus & Giroux, 1957), 124 (hereafter cited as *M&M*).
10 *M&M*, 184.
11 *CS*, 503.
12 *CS*, 506.
13 *CS*, 507.
14 *CS*, 507–8.
15 *CS*, 508.
16 *CS*, 508.
17 *CS*, 450.
18 *CS*, 473.
19 *CS*, 480.
20 *CS*, 470.
21 *CS*, 474.
22 The mirroring of Rufus' foot and Sheppard's interior is a good example of how O'Connor uses disability with complexity. Disability serves as a metaphor for sin, yet the larger meaning critiques negative social perceptions of disability. Congruent with a disability perspective, Rufus does not allow his clubbed foot to define him. He sees with great clarity that his spiritual self is not subservient to his disability. Also in line with a disability perspective, the story is critical of Sheppard's perception of Rufus that totalizes Rufus according to the disability. Even where O'Connor does use the disability as a metaphor, she does not

use it for the boy's sin, as Sheppard and the reader might expect, and as O'Connor does use Joy/Hulga's disability in "Good Country People." Rather Sheppard's medicalized perspective is what mirrors the foot as a monstrosity. O'Connor thus uses disability as a metaphor to condemn explicitly the medical perspective of disability. Sheppard's sentimentality and reaction to the clubbed foot is the story's true grotesque and, in O'Connor's view, the real sin.

23 CS, 482.

24 Concerning O'Connor's statement that she must make corruption believable before grace can be meaningful, Kilcourse writes, "There is no better compass to orient us to her fiction." George Kilcourse, *Flannery O'Connor's Religious Imagination* (New York: Paulist Press, 2001), 28.

25 Roney provides an example of a disability- and literature-studies critic that gets this correct. In sharp contrast to the way Dobrott reads O'Connor's use of disability in "Good Country People" as a perhaps unconscious unleashing of her feelings about her lack of self-sufficiency, Roney instead provides a sensitive critique of O'Connor's use of disability to portray sin, a use that includes more than an aesthetic/metaphorical reading. She writes, "Her family's and her small-town southern culture's habits of 'politeness' meant that the primary avenue for direct exploration of the implications of these ideas and the conflicting strains of Catholicism was through her fiction, and there the disabled bodies explode from the page in a violent attack on the idea that they might be any less or more deserving than the able-bodied in God's view. Since everyone is guilty of sin, she seems to say, sin cannot be some final cause of illness and pain; rather it is only one version of the fallen state of humankind in general." Lisa C. Roney, "Beyond the Pale: Chronic Illness, Disability, and Difference in the Fiction of Katherine Anne Porter, Carson McCullers, and Flannery O'Connor" (Ph.D. diss., Pennsylvania State University, 2001), 15. Roney's perspective acknowledges the metaphorical value of Hulga's missing leg and uses that value, as I believe O'Connor did, to critique the modern obsession with self-sufficiency. Dobrott's reading ignores a disability-studies perspective, while Roney's is sensitive to a perspective that both raises the sociopolitical concerns of disability and understands the aesthetic value disability carries in literature.

26 M&M, 99.

27 Concerning Manichaeism being heretical in O'Connor's view, Thomas Haddox writes about a conversation, in letters, O'Connor had concerning dramatizing a heresy in "Parker's Back." He writes, "O'Connor then clarified what Gordon had meant in a follow-up letter of 25

July: 'No Caroline didn't mean the tattoos were the heresy. Sarah Ruth was the heretic—the notion that you can worship in pure spirit' (p. 594). These passages provide the kernel of all 'sacramental' readings of the story, holding up Parker's delight in the flesh—including the tattoos—against Sarah Ruth's Manichean equation of God with spirit." Haddox, "'Something Haphazard and Botched': Flannery O'Connor's Critique of the Visual in 'Parker's Back.'" *Mississippi Quarterly* 57, no. 3 (2004): 408.

28 Flannery O'Connor, *The Habit of Being* (New York: Farrar, Straus & Giroux, 1980), 173 (hereafter cited as *HB*).

29 Kilcourse, *Religious Imagination*, 115.

30 Kilcourse, *Religious Imagination*, 116.

31 This is the thesis of Christina Bieber Lake's book *The Incarnational Art of Flannery O'Connor* (Macon, Ga.: Mercer University Press, 2005).

32 *M&M*, 111.

33 Kilcourse, *Religious Imagination*, 116; emphasis added.

34 Flannery O'Connor, *Collected Works* (New York: Literary Classics of the United States, 1988), 1182 (hereafter referred to as *CW*).

35 *M&M*, 35. Ralph Wood writes that "in our time at least, an anguishing self-knowledge is the prime requisite for recognizing the Gospel of God. Nothing less than this glad grace is what most of [O'Connor's] protagonists find." Wood, *The Comedy of Redemption: Christian Faith and Comic Vision in Four American Novelists* (Notre Dame: University of Notre Dame Press, 1988), 81.

36 *M&M*, 167.

37 *CS*, 245.

38 *CS*, 246.

39 *CS*, 248.

40 *CS*, 248.

41 Thomas writes concerning the story's ending, "For the girl, [the hermaphrodite] has effected a redemption of sorts, a realization and acceptance of human flaw, disabilities and weaknesses. However, the townspeople's rejection of the hermaphrodite indicates embarrassment and a denial of the imperfection of humans. . . . The ugliness of the hermaphrodite offends the community, but that very ugliness becomes a source of grace, in that this person accepts its adverse physical condition and draws the girl closer to an acceptance of the physically undesirable." Wendy Thomas, "More Instructive Than a Long Trip to Europe: The Effects of Lupus on Flannery O'Connor's Short Stories" (Master's thesis, University of New Brunswick, 1997), 41.

42   Thomas notes the cousins "are too involved in trying to look appealing to contemplate anything spiritual. They have perfect and young bodies; disease and deformity are not a concern." Thomas, "More Instructive," 39.

43   *HB*, 90.

44   *HB*, 124.

45   *CS*, 357.

46   *CS*, 370.

47   *CS*, 364.

48   *CS*, 358; emphasis in original.

49   *CS*, 378.

50   *CS*, 377.

51   *CS*, 382.

52   Steven Watkins, "Teilhard de Chardin's View of Diminishment and the Late Stories of Flannery O'Connor" (Ph.D. diss., University of Texas at Arlington, 2005), 87.

53   Wood writes about this: "Asbury's body will not be purified by the nonfatal illness he is so disappointed to have contracted, thus being deprived of the death that would mark 'his greatest triumph' over his smothering mother. Instead, his enduring chills and fevers will require him to live in lasting dependence upon her. But there is at least a chance that he will find the purity of heart that beholds God himself. For at the end of the story, Asbury enters the purgatorial life that has the power to cleanse all his unrighteousness, whether racial or filial, as the Holy Ghost descends upon him—not as a dove carrying the olive branch or peace but as a fierce bird bearing the icicle of judgment." Ralph Wood, *Flannery O'Connor and the Christ-Haunted South* (Grand Rapids: Eerdmans, 2004), 116.

54   *CS*, 375.

Chapter Three

1   Luke 1:29-38.

2   William Wordsworth, "The Virgin," in *The Ecclesiastical Sonnets of William Wordsworth* (New Haven: Yale University Press, 1922), 151. Thanks to J. Morriss for suggesting this phrase.

3   Heb 5:8-9 (NIV) reads, "Although he was a son, he learned obedience from what he suffered and, once made perfect, he became the source of eternal salvation for all who obey him."

4   Flannery O'Connor, *The Complete Stories of Flannery O'Connor* (New York: Noonday, 1971), 147 (hereafter cited as *CS*).

5   *CS*, 149.

6   CS, 150.
7   I am here parroting the work of Hans Reinders.
8   Flannery O'Connor, *Mystery and Manners* (New York: Farrar, Straus & Giroux, 1957), 165–66 (hereafter cited as *M&M*).
9   Phil 2:6-8 (NIV).
10 See in particular Jurgen Moltmann's chapter section entitled "The healing power of Jesus lies in his ability to suffer" in "Liberate Yourselves by Accepting One Another" in *Human Disability and the Service of God*, ed. Nancy Eisland and Don Saliers (Nashville: Abingdon, 1998).
11 Flannery O'Connor, *The Habit of Being* (New York: Farrar, Straus & Giroux, 1980), 354 (hereafter cited as *HB*).
12 *HB*, 97.
13 CS, 171.
14 CS, 168.
15 CS, 172.
16 CS, 173.
17 Ralph Wood, "The Scandalous Baptism of Harry Ashfield: Flannery O'Connor's 'The River,'" in *Inside the Church of Flannery O'Connor: Sacrament, Sacramental, and the Sacred in Her Fiction*, ed. Joanne Halleran McMullen and Jon Parrish Peede (Macon, Ga.: Mercer University Press, 2007), 189.
18 This is an argument Wood makes very clear.
19 *M&M*, 226.
20 *M&M*, 226.
21 See Christina Bieber Lake, "Mary Ann's Face and Parker's Back: The Grotesque Body Under Construction," in *The Incarnational Art of Flannery O'Connor* (Macon, Ga.: Mercer University Press, 2005), for an analysis along these lines.
22 Caleb Dulis also makes this connection between Sheppard and Rayber quite nicely. He notes O'Connor's philosophical indictment of the "usefulness" of their shared modernity. Agreeing with the point I will be making here, Dulis writes, "Love is directly opposed to usefulness in either of these stories. The ontology of modernity is made explicitly to oppose a world-view that embraces the other. Indeed, the acceptance of otherness threatens to lead to the Ultimate Other embodied in the Christian God and thus threatens the stability of a materialist understanding. Each character's refusal to acknowledge love and the 'other' as the object of love in favor of personal conceptions of the good leaves them unprepared for the dissolution of reality." Caleb Dulis,

"'Everything Off Balance': Flannery O'Connor's Theology of Cultural Antagonism" (Master's thesis, University of Virginia, 2005), available online at http://xroads.virginia.edu/~ma05/dulis/fo/beyond1.html.

23 Flannery O'Connor, *The Violent Bear It Away* (New York: Farrar, Straus & Cudahy, 1955), 4 (hereafter cited as *TVBIA*).

24 Wood references this quote as "accents of nihilistic autarky." My argument in this paragraph follows Wood's suggestion that "O'Connor reveals modern notions of autonomy have satanic implications." Ralph Wood, *Flannery O'Connor and the Christ-Haunted South* (Grand Rapids: Eerdmans, 2004), 186, 188.

25 Wood notes the theological history of the initial freedom sin offers as opposed to the seemingly restrictive obedience God demands. Yet God's demand is actually the freedom to choose, whereas sin and rebellion restrict choice more and more as they are pursued. He offers the analogy of taking illegal drugs that at first seem to open entirely new and wonderful ways of experiencing reality, yet quickly become abusive in their demands upon and ravishing of the person.

26 *TVBIA*, 60.

27 *M&M*, 209.

28 *TVBIA*, 60.

29 *TVBIA*, 168.

30 Bieber Lake writes, "*The Violent Bear It Away* signals, more than any other work, O'Connor's shift in sensibility with regard to the possibilities of the grotesque. Most of the grotesques in her early career signify lack, the absence of something good in characters, the perverse result of the fall. These grotesques can only challenge by repulsion, even when we find that what we are repulsed by is ourselves. But Bishop and the later grotesques signify the presence of Being in being, the divinely created core of humanity that can be seen in spite of our fallen nature. O'Connor called such grotesquerie 'the face of good under construction.' These grotesques mysteriously attract us even *as* they repel us; they bid us to ask questions, and they suggest beauty of another order entirely." Bieber Lake, *Incarnational Art*, 142; emphasis original.

31 Rudolf Otto, *The Idea of the Holy* (Oxford: Oxford University Press, 1923).

32 *TVBIA*, 19.

33 *TVBIA*, 195.

34 *TVBIA*, 194.

35 *TVBIA*, 32.

36 *TVBIA*, 33–34.

37 *TVBIA*, 34.

38   Ladislava Khailova, "'Where the Average White Male Scored in the Imbecile Range': Changing Paradigms of Mental Retardation in Twentieth-Century Southern Fiction" (Ph.D. diss., University of South Carolina, 2004), 148.

39   As George Kilcourse writes, "In Rayber's world, both Mason and Bishop are 'freaks,' the one a freak of nature, the other a freak of religious superstition." Kilcourse, *Flannery O'Connor's Religious Imagination* (New York: Paulist Press, 2001), 236.

40   *TVBIA*, 42. On p. 44, one of the voices attempts to convince Tarwater that Mason is crazy, telling him, "he was crazy! He was crazy! That's the long and short of it, he was crazy!"

41   *TVBIA*, 56.

42   As Ted Spivey explains, Tarwater is an everyman. "Divided between the tar of death and the water of life, Tarwater seeks at once to throw off the life power within himself in order to enjoy his own desires and pleasures and at the same time finds that he cannot free himself of an inherited awareness of the springs of divine existence." Spivey, *Flannery O'Connor: The Woman, the Thinker, the Visionary* (Macon, Ga.: Mercer University Press, 1997), 138.

43   Rayber's struggle is similar. Spivey explains, "As a Cartesian and a son of the eighteenth-century Enlightenment, he is at war within himself—split between his unrepressable love and his desire to conform his life and other lives to a system of knowledge that has no explanation or place for love." Spivey, *Flannery O'Connor*, 138.

44   *TVBIA*, 112.

45   *TVBIA*, 113.

46   *TVBIA*, 113.

47   This is Bieber Lake's interpretation. She therefore takes the statement of Bishop being in the image of God at face value and finds it puzzling that other critics have viewed Bishop negatively, notably "Baumgaertner's argument that Bishop is a manifestation of the metaphor of the dead word." Bieber Lake, *Incarnational Art*, 147n.

48   This is Ralph Wood's interpretation of the scene. He writes, "This brain-stunted child proves, according to Rayber's reasoning, that the universe is an unsponsored and undirected flux, the product of absurd chance. If there is a God, Rayber concludes, he is a ham-fisted creator formed in Bishop's imbecilic image." Wood, *Christ-Haunted South*, 195.

49   *TVBIA*, 113–14.

50   *TVBIA*, 113.

51   Ted Spivey argues that in writing *The Violent Bear it Away*, O'Connor was concerned with the isolation created by modern philosophy. He

writes concerning the old prophet Mason, "The humor of his life is revealed in the occasional absurdity of his attempting to live out beliefs that nearly everyone in the modern world regards as largely meaningless. Yet the novel makes it quite clear that through the mystery of his belief and his receiving of grace, Mason Tarwater in fact escapes the condition of the haunted mind which goes mad because of isolation and obsession. Tarwater is able to love, and through love his life, absurd though it sometimes is, becomes fruitful for others. His 'violent' and forceful seizure of the Kingdom of God makes possible fructification in the lives of others." Spivey, *Flannery O'Connor*, 131.

52 *TVBIA*, 9.

53 Khailova argues that O'Connor portrays disability in her fiction from a premodern viewpoint that refuses the medical perspective of disability as a problem to be fixed. "In such a revival of pre-scientific modes of viewing disability, the mental states of Bishop Rayber (*The Violent Bear It Away*) and Lucynell Crater ("The Life You Save May Be Your Own") are presented as a consequence of human corruption, but also mainly as its conceptual opposite: a protection from the disbelief and superfluous self-assertion of a typical modern secularist." She continues, "In their self-effacement, they perform the function of God's corrective agents sent to reform all the proud excessive individualists." Khailova, "Average White Male," 143.

54 *M&M*, 227.

Chapter Four

1 Quoted in Brad Gooch, *Flannery: A Life of Flannery O'Connor* (New York: Little, Brown, 2009), 228.

2 Luke 19:37-38.

3 Luke 19:41.

4 Luke 19:42.

5 Flannery O'Connor, *The Habit of Being* (New York: Farrar, Straus & Giroux, 1980), 354 (hereafter cited as *HB*).

6 See http://www.sacredheartmilledgeville.org/history.html, accessed April 10, 2012.

7 Gooch, *Flannery*, 26–27.

8 *HB*, 136.

9 *HB*, 137.

10 Flannery O'Connor, *The Complete Stories of Flannery O'Connor* (New York: Noonday, 1971), 133 (hereafter cited as *CS*).

11 Quoted in Gooch, *Flannery* , 72.

12 Col 1:24 (NRSV).
13 My method throughout this book has been to apply a disability perspective to O'Connor and her fiction. I have attempted not to impose this perspective upon her from the outside, but instead to view her through the lens of disability and note how her theological and literary perspectives were affected by her disability. I have found in my study that a disability perspective has much to offer those interested in O'Connor's work and life but also that O'Connor has much to offer disability studies.
14 Deborah Creamer notes, "The perspective of the medical model is that the body is a biological machine that functions to a greater or lesser extent. Disability, then, is located solely within the body, with no appeal to societal or environmental factors. It is an individual rather than societal condition." Creamer, *Disability and Christian Theology: Embodied Limits and Constructive Possibilities* (New York: Oxford University Press, 2009), 24. Ato Quayson agrees and explores some of the psychological effects: "The notion of disability as personal tragedy places people with disabilities within a narrative in which accommodation to the impairment is squarely their own responsibility or that of their families. The medical and social systems are then tasked with corrective, ameliorative, or reprimanding roles, reminding the person with disability to 'get a grip' and take charge of the process of his or her self-improvement and adjustment. Indeed, in the medical model, the person with disability is placed under an obligation to want to get well, his or her multiple social roles, of parent, worker, spouse, and so on being suspended temporarily in exchange for a sign of strenuous effort toward improvement." Quayson, *Aesthetic Nervousness: Disability and the Crisis of Representation* (New York: Columbia University Press, 2007), 2.
15 Christopher Newell writes, "Disability, in this [medical] model, is almost universally a negative analysis because it concentrates on the idea of disability as a loss of function in one way or another. Disability is, therefore, 'a lack, a deficit, an inability . . . disability is a problem that is experienced by an individual; it represents a deviation from a state of normality because of an impairment.'" Newell, "Disabled Theologies and the Journeys of Liberation to Where Our Names Appear," *Feminist Theology* 15, no. 3 (2007): 324. Newell is quoting Roy McCloughry and Wayne Morris, *Making a World of Difference: Christian Reflections on Disability* (London: SPCK, 2002), 9.
16 Thomson goes on to write, "Not only does this definition of the female as a 'mutilated male' inform later depictions of woman as diminished

man, but it also arranges somatic diversity into a hierarchy of value that assigns completeness to some bodies and devidiency [*sic*] to others." Rosemarie Garland Thomson, *Extraordinary Bodies: Figuring Disability in American Culture and Literature* (New York: Columbia University Press, 1997), 20.

17 Christopher Newell argues along these lines in the following paragraph, ending with a move toward theology that I will later also make: "Despite the enormous development of medical services, particularly in the West, that seek to 'treat' the diagnosed disability of a person, and the benefits that have accrued to individuals, families and communities, the idea of the disability itself as a medical problem to be fixed has effectively professionalized the idea of disability and marginalized and stigmatized persons with disabilities. A deep rooted dualism or dualisms have demarcated the professional from the person, the disability from the body and mind within which it resides, the them who are disabled from the us who are not and the power and control to treat and intervene from the voice of those who find themselves treated and invaded. Therefore, the very act of reflecting upon the nature and experience of disability, even as we attempt to describe a purely medical model, if such a pure model exists, plunges us into deep waters of theological tradition and existentialism." Newell, "Disabled Theologies," 325.

18 Creamer notes, "The medical model has the principle of normalization at its core, attempting to modify, repair, or relocate individuals with disabilities until they are congruent with societal expectations of normalcy and acceptability." Creamer, *Disability and Christian Theology*, 24.

19 Jackie Leach Scully puts it succinctly, "The social models' most fundamental criticism of the medical model is that it wrongly locates 'the problem' of disability in the individual and neglects the social and structural." Scully, "Drawing Lines, Crossing Lines: Ethics and the Challenge of Disabled Embodiment," *Feminist Theology* 11, no. 3 (2003): 266. However, while arguing the social constructedness of disability, one must be careful not to swing the pendulum too far. Johnson Fan Cheu writes, "I do not mean to claim here that there is no biological basis for impairment; rather I am suggesting that what constitutes an 'impairment' and an 'impaired body' must also be understood to be culturally constructed." Fan Cheu, "Disabling Cure in Twentieth-Century America: Disability, Identity, Literature and Culture" (Ph.D. diss., Ohio State University, 2003), 14.

20 A noted professor and priest, Henri Nouwen, spent the end of his life at a L'Arche community outside Toronto. He chronicles his helping and being helped by a severely disabled man named Adam Arnett in a book entitled *Adam: God's Beloved* (Maryknoll: Orbis, 1997).

21 Stanley Hauerwas writes, "God's face is the face of the retarded; God's body is the body of the retarded; God's being is that of the retarded. For the God we Christians must learn to worship is not a God of self-sufficient power, a God who in self-possession needs no one; rather ours is a God who needs a people, who needs a Son. The Absoluteness of being or power is not a work of the God we have come to know through the cross." Hauerwas, *Suffering Presence: Theological Reflections on Medicine, the Mentally Handicapped, and the Church* (Notre Dame: University of Notre Dame Press, 1986), 178.

22 Burton Cooper writes, "Thus, human 'ableness' provides us with the image to think about God's power." Cooper, "The Disabled God," *Theology Today* 49, no. 2 (1992): 180.

23 Flannery O'Connor, *The Violent Bear It Away* (New York: Farrar, Straus & Cudahy, 1955), 33–34 (hereafter cited as *TVBIA*).

24 *TVBIA*, 113.

25 Cooper, "Disabled God," 180.

26 *TVBIA*, 113.

27 Cooper, "Disabled God," 176.

28 Matt 5:48.

29 John 20:27.

30 World Council of Churches, "A Church of All and For All: An Interim Statement," *International Review of Missions* 93, no. 370/371 (2004): 512.

31 In place of using autonomy as the base definition of selfhood, a more authentic definition is provided by Jennie Weiss Block: "the extent to which we are known and loved by others and the extent to which we are able to love, is the extent to which we exist." Block, *Copious Hosting: A Theology of Access for People with Disabilities* (London: Continuum, 2002), 260.

32 Nancy Eisland, *The Disabled God: Toward a Liberatory Theology of Disability* (Nashville: Abingdon, 1994), 103. Just before this quote, she notes, "The disabled God is God for whom interdependence is not a possibility to be willed from a position of power, but a necessary condition for life."

33 Thomas Reynolds, *Vulnerable Communion: A Theology of Disability and Hospitality* (Grand Rapids: Brazos, 2008), 117–18.

34 See Gen 1:26, 28.

35   Helen Betenbaugh, "Disability: A Lived Theology," *Theology Today* 57, no. 2 (2000): 208. For another perspective, see Samuel Kabue's "Disability and the Healing Mission of the Church," where he examines the nature in which many of the healing narratives in the gospels include and even prioritize the acceptance of the individual back into the community, in *International Review of Missions* 95, nos. 576–77 (2006): 112–16; emphasis original.

36   Betenbaugh, "Disability," 209.

37   As Nancy Eisland puts it in *The Disabled God*, "Justice for people with disabilities requires that the theological and ritual foundations of the church be shaken" (111).

38   Betenbaugh, "Disability," 208.

39   In his book *Vulnerable Communion*, Thomas Reynolds writes, "This is not a moral lesson that people with disabilities teach non-disabled persons; it is rather an opening to the humanity of disabled and non-disabled persons alike" (107).

40   As Reynolds succinctly and beautifully puts it, "Vulnerability and dependence is normal." Reynolds, *Vulnerable Communion*, 129.

41   Phil 2:6-8 (NRSV; emphasis added).

42   Heidi Latsky, "GIMP Background—Director's Notes," GIMP Project, http://www.thegimpproject.com/gimp/ brief/background/.

43   Latsky, "Director's Notes."

44   John Swinton led this research group, and he reflected on the project in an article entitled "The Body of Christ has Down's Syndrome: Theological Reflections on Vulnerability, Disability, and Graceful Communities," *Journal of Pastoral Theology* 13, no. 2 (2003): 67, available online at http://www.abdn.ac.uk/cshad/TheBodyofChristHasDown Syndrome.htm.

45   Swinton, "Body of Christ," 67; emphasis original. Swinton uses Frances Young's term *transvaluation* from an unpublished paper presented at a conference for theologians held at "La Ferme" in the community of L'Arche in Trosly-Breuil, France, in December of 2002.

46   Swinton, "Body of Christ," 71.

47   Swinton, "Body of Christ," 72.

48   Swinton, "Body of Christ," 73.

49   Swinton, "Body of Christ," 75.

50   Gretchen Dobrott, "Coping with Lupus: Images of Illness in the Short Stories of Flannery O'Connor" (paper presented at the 6th Global Conference of Making Sense of: Health, Illness and Disease at Mansfield College, Oxford, July 2007), 8, available online at http://www.inter-disciplinary.net/ptb/mso/hid/hid6/dobrott%20paper.pdf.

51 Dobrott, "Coping with Lupus," 7. Other scholars have made simi-
    lar suggestions to that of Dobrott. Andre Bliekanstan believes that
    O'Connor's literature is primarily a desperate cry against the cruelties
    of life in the face of a deteriorating long-term disease. See Bliekan-
    stan, "The Heresy of Flannery O'Connor," in *Critical Essays on Flan-
    nery O'Connor*, ed. Melvin Friedman and Beverly Lyon Clark (Boston:
    G. K. Hall, 1985).

52 Dobrott makes this argument again when commenting on "reli-
    gious" interpretations: "Those who interpret her stories from a reli-
    gious stance would likely support the idea that her disabled, ill, and
    mutilated characters are instrumental and serve as one of the primary
    means of reaching her didactic aims. Indeed, there is no disputing that
    O'Connor makes strategic use of the 'abnormal,' or 'non-normate'
    body. By accentuating the otherness of her characters, she is employing
    a powerful rhetorical device which strengthens her message and aids
    in the transmission of her argument. However, along with a smaller
    group of women scholars, I suggest that the recurrence of illness-
    and disability-related images—her shouting to the deaf and drawing
    startling figures for the near-blind—could have also been a way of
    venting her frustration toward her imminent death and her personal
    circumstances. For not only did she have to endure the symptoms of
    lupus, but she had to depend almost entirely on her mother, as well,
    while living under physically restrictive conditions." Dobrott, "Coping
    with Lupus," 4. Again we can note Dobrott's misconceived assump-
    tion that O'Connor despised being dependent on her mother. Apart
    from this, however, Dobrott makes a very good point, and most reli-
    gious interpretations, and in fact most non-religious interpretations,
    do consider her portrayals of disabled, ill, and mutilated characters as
    instrumental in serving her religious ends. Dobrott herself concedes
    this was O'Connor's purpose and that the characters function thusly
    within the stories. Where we differ is that she concludes O'Connor's
    grotesques reflect her frustration with not being self-sufficient, and I
    think the weight of evidence points in a very different direction.

53 *HB*, 581.

54 In discussing O'Connor's disability with Bill Sessions, who knew her
    well and visited her at Andalusia on numerous occasions, he has com-
    mented to me multiple times that O'Connor never complained about
    her disability or felt sorry for herself.

55 *HB*, 286.

56 *HB*, 509.

57   As Claire Kahane puts it, "with a rare gusto that sparkled on the page and gained the reader's complicity, she punished any characters deluded enough to believe in their autonomy. The idea that a protagonist could say, as Hazel Motes does, 'I'm doing all right by myself,' was a provocation and an anathema. Invariably O'Connor exploded such an assertion through her wit as well as through her plot. Stripping her characters bare of any illusion of independence, she shocked them— and her readers—into a terrifying awareness of their vulnerability and their need." Kahane, "The Re-vision of Rage: Flannery O'Connor and Me," *Massachusetts Review* 46, no. 3 (2005): 442, 439–61.
58   *HB*, 90.
59   Peter Huggins, "Flannery O'Connor at Lourdes," *Anglican Theological Review* 90, no. 2 (2008): 350.
60   Flannery O'Connor, *Mystery and Manners* (New York: Farrar, Straus & Giroux, 1957), 226–27.

Postscript

1   Thomson writes, "From folktales and classical myths to modern and postmodern 'grotesques,' the disabled body is almost always a freakish spectacle presented by the mediating narrative voice." Rosemarie Garland Thomson, *Extraordinary Bodies: Figuring Disability in American Culture and Literature* (New York: Columbia University Press, 1997), 10.
2   In her seminal work on representations of disability in literature, Thomson mentions O'Connor's work twice, both times as examples of negative representations. One of her references to O'Connor comes in her discussion of how society labels anomaly as dangerous. She writes, "Like the monsters who are their cousins, disabled characters with power virtually always represent a dangerous force unleashed on the social order, as attested by Flannery O'Connor's one-armed villain Tom Shiftlet. . . . Because these characters operate as embodiments of an unnamed, profound peril, the narrative resolution is almost always to contain that threat by killing or disempowering the disabled character. The logic that governs this cultural narrative, then, is that eliminating the anomaly neutralizes the danger." Thomson, *Extraordinary Bodies*, 36. She also references O'Connor on p. 12, noting the purposefully and necessarily negative representation that Joy/Hulga provides: "If Flannery O'Connor's Hulga Hopewell were pretty, cheerful, and one-legged instead of ugly and bitter, 'Good Country People' would fail."
3   Ladislava Khailova notes the surprising amount of disabled persons within Southern literature, but also the surprising lack of recognition

amongst critics of disabled persons as a distinguishing feature of Southern fiction. She writes, "Thus far, Southern literary scholarship has almost exclusively produced aesthetic interpretations of characters who are one-armed, one-legged, and deaf-mute, hunchbacked, insane, and retarded. In other words, disability in Southern texts has been predominantly interpreted metaphorically, as an element of the Southern grotesque and the Southern gothic traditions or merely as a literary symbol of the human condition or character." Khailova, "'Where the Average White Male Scored in the Imbecile Range': Changing Paradigms of Mental Retardation in Twentieth-Century Southern Fiction" (Ph.D. diss., University of South Carolina, 2004), 2.

4   Johnson Fan Cheu notes, "As many Disability Studies scholars have pointed out, representations of disability in our literary and media culture are almost always negative, tied up in notions of the disabled body as lacking, diseased, sick, different, inherently 'Other.'" Fan Cheu, "Disabling Cure in Twentieth-Century America: Disability, Identity, Literature and Culture" (Ph.D. diss., Ohio State University, 2003), 4.

5   Flannery O'Connor, *Mystery and Manners* (New York: Farrar, Straus & Giroux, 1957), 34 (hereafter cited as *M&M*).

6   Flannery O'Connor, *The Habit of Being* (New York: Farrar, Straus & Giroux, 1980), 79.

7   O'Connor scholarship has engaged the politics of race and sex, but since it has discussed the grotesque in almost exclusively aesthetic language, it has largely ignored the sociopolitical realities of disability in her stories, as well as the sociopolitical realities of O'Connor's own disability. For example, Lisa Roney points out that Patricia Yaeger's book *Dirt and Desire: Reconstructing Southern Women's Writing, 1930–1990* "focuses almost exclusively on the images of bodies and the grotesque," and argues these images are metaphorical expressions of racial violence in the South. Yet Yaeger never references O'Connor's own illness and disability, causing Roney to note that "it seems problematic to discuss O'Connor's use of 'sawed-off, deregulated bodies' without even mentioning that the damage O'Connor experienced in her own body was not caused by racist violence, but by a ravaging illness." Roney, "Beyond the Pale: Chronic Illness, Disability, and Difference in the Fiction of Katherine Anne Porter, Carson McCullers, and Flannery O'Connor" (Ph.D. diss., Pennsylvania State University, 2001), 68.

8   Though the task is difficult, a few voices have begun to consider the realities of disability in O'Connor's life and works. Such consideration is thoughtfully done by Kathleen Anne Patterson in her dissertation, "Representations of Disability in Mid-Twentieth-Century Southern

Fiction: From Metaphor to Social Construction" (Ph.D. diss., University of California, Santa Barbara, 1998). Also helpful is Wendy Thomas' "More Instructive Than a Long Trip to Europe: The Effects of Lupus on Flannery O'Connor's Short Stories" (Master's thesis, University of New Brunswick, 1997);and Johnson Fan Cheu's dissertation "Disabling Cure," previously cited.

9   Flannery O'Connor, *The Complete Stories of Flannery O'Connor* (New York: Noonday, 1971), 151–52 (hereafter cited as CS).

10   CS, 149.

11   In their book *Narrative Prosthesis: Disability and the Dependencies of Discourse* (Ann Arbor: University of Michigan Press, 2001), David Mitchell and Sharon Snyder argue there is an overabundance of disability within literature.

12   *M&M*, 99.

13   *M&M*, 45.

14   Roney provides an example of a critique sensitive both to metaphorical meaning and to sociopolitical concerns. Writing about Porter, McCullers, and O'Connor at the end of her introduction, she notes, "Each of them viewed the debates that raged about race, genetics, superiority, and the public good from a perspective shaped by illness and disability. In the fiction of each there are signs that they understood the overlaps between arguments about the status of African Americans and those about the 'unfit.' Each of them, like their region more widely, struggled with the implications of hereditarian theories and policies, with the social challenges raised by the existence of physical imperfection, and with such imperfections' nagging intimations of human mortality." She comments both on how the writers were shaped by their own illnesses and on the metaphorical "intimations" of imperfection that are universal but held particular political significance for these disabled authors living near the end of the eugenics period in which society's "weak" were blamed for social ills and then confined or even killed in an attempt to bolster the human gene pool. Roney, "Beyond the Pale," 69.

Bibliography

Askin, Denise. "Anagogical Vision and Comedic Form in Flannery O'Connor: The Reasonable Use of the Unreasonable." *Renascence* 57, no. 1 (2004): 47–62.

Baumgaertner, Jill. "'The Meaning Is in You': Flannery O'Connor in Her Letters." *Christian Century* 104, no. 39 (1987): 1172–76.

Betenbaugh, Helen. "Disability: A Lived Theology." *Theology Today* 57, no. 2 (2000): 203–10.

Bieber Lake, Christina. *The Incarnational Art of Flannery O'Connor.* Macon, Ga.: Mercer University Press, 2005.

———. "Vocation through Limitation: Flannery O'Connor's Life of Faith." *The Cresset* 71, no. 4 (2008): 6–13.

Bliekanstan, Andre. "The Heresy of Flannery O'Connor." *Critical Essays on Flannery O'Connor.* Edited by Melvin Friedman and Beverly Lyon Clark. Boston: G. K. Hall, 1985.

Block, Jennie Weiss. *Copious Hosting: A Theology of Access for People with Disabilities.* London: Continuum, 2002.

Brueggemann, Brenda Jo, and Marian E. Lupo, eds. *Disability and/in Prose.* New York: Routledge, 2008.

Cash, Jean. *Flannery O'Connor: A Life.* Knoxville: University of Tennessee Press, 2002.

Charlton, James I. *Nothing about Us without Us: Disability, Oppression, and Empowerment.* Berkeley: University of California Press, 1998.

Cohen, Jeffrey. *Monster Theory: Reading Culture.* Minneapolis: University of Minnesota Press, 1996.

Cooper, Burton. "The Disabled God." *Theology Today* 49, no. 2 (1992): 173–82.

Creamer, Deborah. *Disability and Christian Theology: Embodied Limits and Constructive Possibilities.* New York: Oxford University Press, 2009.

Davis, Lennard. *Bending over Backwards: Disability, Dismodernism, and Other Difficult Positions.* New York: New York University Press, 2003.

DeVries, Dawn. "Creation, Handicappism, and the Community of Differing Abilities." In *Reconstructing Christian Theology*, edited by Rebecca Chöpp and Mark L. Taylor, 124–40. Minneapolis: Augsburg, 1994.

Dobrott, Gretchen. "Coping with Lupus: Images of Illness in the Short Stories of Flannery O'Connor." Paper presented at the 6th Global Conference of Making Sense of: Health, Illness and Disease at Mansfield College, Oxford, July 2007. Available online at http://www.inter-disciplinary.net/ptb/mso/hid/hid6/dobrott%20paper.pdf.

Dolmage, Jay. "Between the Valley and the Field: Metaphor and Disability." In Brueggemann and Lupo, *Disability and/in Prose*, 98–109.

Dulis, Caleb. "'Everything Off Balance': Flannery O'Connor's Theology of Cultural Antagonism." Master's thesis, University of Virginia, 2005. Available online at http://xroads.virginia.edu/~ma05/dulis/fo/beyond1.html.

Eisland, Nancy. "Barriers and Bridges: Relating the Disability Rights Movement and Religious Organizations." In Eisland and Saliers, *Human Disability*, 200–229.

———. *The Disabled God: Toward a Liberatory Theology of Disability.* Nashville: Abingdon, 1994.

Eisland, Nancy, and Don E. Saliers, eds. *Human Disability and the Service of God: Reassessing Religious Practice.* Nashville: Abingdon, 1998.

Fan Cheu, Johnson. "Disabling Cure in Twentieth-Century America: Disability, Identity, Literature and Culture." Ph.D. diss., Ohio State University, 2003.

Fiedler, Leslie A. *Pity and Fear: Myths and Images of the Disabled in Literature Old and New.* New York: International Center for the Disabled, 1982.

González-Andrieu, Cecilia. "Garcia Lorca as Theologian: The Method and Practice of Interlacing the Arts and Theology." Ph.D. diss., Graduate Theological Union, March 2007.

Gooch, Brad. *Flannery: A Life of Flannery O'Connor.* New York: Little, Brown, 2009.

Haddox, Thomas. "'Something Haphazard and Botched': Flannery O'Connor's Critique of the Visual in 'Parker's Back.'" *Mississippi Quarterly* 57, no. 3 (2004): 407–21.

Hauerwas, Stanley. *Suffering Presence: Theological Reflections on Medicine, the Mentally Handicapped, and the Church.* Notre Dame: University of Notre Dame Press, 1986.

Hayward, Sally. "'Those Who Cannot Work:' An Exploration of Disabled Men and Masculinity in Henry Mayhew's *London Labour and the London Poor.*" In Brueggemann and Lupo, *Disability and/in Prose*, 43–61.

Huggins, Peter. "Flannery O'Connor at Lourdes." *Anglican Theological Review* 90, no. 2 (2008): 350.

Jordan, Michael M. "Flannery O'Connor's Writing: A Guide for the Perplexed." *MA* 47, no. 1 (2005). Available online at http://www.firstprinciplesjournal.com/articles.aspx?article=782&theme=home&page=1&loc=b&type=cttf.

Kabue, Samuel. "Disability and the Healing Mission of the Church." *International Review of Missions* 95, no. 576/577 (2006): 112–16.

Kahane, Claire. "The Re-vision of Rage: Flannery O'Connor and Me." *Massachusetts Review* 46, no. 3 (2005): 439–61.

Khailova, Ladislava. "'Where the Average White Male Scored in the Imbecile Range': Changing Paradigms of Mental Retardation in Twentieth-Century Southern Fiction." Ph.D. diss., University of South Carolina, 2004.

Kilcourse, George. *Flannery O'Connor's Religious Imagination.* New York: Paulist Press, 2001.

Latsky, Heidi. "GIMP Background—Director's Notes." GIMP Project. http://www.thegimpproject.com/gimp/brief/background/.

Lynch, William. *Christ and Apollo: The Dimensions of the Literary Imagination.* New York: Sheed & Ward, 1960.

May, Vivian, and Beth Ferri. "Fixated on Ability: Questioning Ableist Metaphors in Feminist Theories of Resistance." In Brueggemann and Lupo, *Disability and/in Prose,* 110–30.

McCollum, Adele. "Tradition, Folklore, and Disability: A Heritage of Inclusion." In Eisland and Saliers, *Human Disability,* 167–86.

Mitchell, David, and Sharon Snyder. *Narrative Prosthesis: Disability and the Dependencies of Discourse.* Ann Arbor: University of Michigan Press, 2001.

———. "Representation and Its Discontents: The Uneasy Home of Disability in Literature and Film." In *The Handbook of Disability Studies,* edited by Gary Albrecht, Katherine Seelman, and Michael Bury, 195–218. Thousand Oaks, Calif.: Sage Publications, 2001.

Moltmann, Jurgen. "Liberate Yourselves by Accepting One Another." In Eisland and Saliers, *Human Disability,* 105–22.

Newell, Christopher. "Disabled Theologies and the Journeys of Liberation to Where Our Names Appear." *Feminist Theology* 15, no. 3 (2007): 322–45.

Nouwen, Henri. *Adam: God's Beloved.* Maryknoll: Orbis, 1997.

O'Connor, Flannery. *Collected Works.* New York: Literary Classics of the United States, 1988.

———. *The Complete Stories of Flannery O'Connor.* New York: Noonday, 1971.

———. *The Habit of Being.* New York: Farrar, Straus & Giroux, 1980.

———. *Mystery and Manners.* New York: Farrar, Straus & Giroux, 1957.

———. *The Violent Bear It Away.* New York: Farrar, Straus & Cudahy, 1955.

Otto, Rudolf. *The Idea of the Holy.* Oxford: Oxford University Press, 1923.

Patterson, Barbara. "Redeemed Bodies: Fullness of Life." In Eisland and Saliers, *Human Disability,* 123–43.

Patterson, Kathleen Anne. "Representations of Disability in Mid-Twentieth-Century Southern Fiction: From Metaphor to Social

Construction." Ph.D. diss., University of California, Santa Barbara, 1998.

Profitt, Jennifer. "Lupus and Corticosteroid Imagery in the Works of Flannery O'Connor." *Flannery O'Connor Bulletin* 26–27 (2000): 75–91.

Quayson, Ato. *Aesthetic Nervousness: Disability and the Crisis of Representation.* New York: Columbia University Press, 2007.

Reinders, Hans. *Receiving the Gift of Friendship: Profound Disability, Theological Anthropology, and Ethics.* Grand Rapids: Eerdmans, 2008.

Reynolds, Thomas. *Vulnerable Communion: A Theology of Disability and Hospitality.* Grand Rapids: Brazos, 2008.

Roney, Lisa C. "Beyond the Pale: Chronic Illness, Disability, and Difference in the Fiction of Katherine Anne Porter, Carson McCullers, and Flannery O'Connor." Ph.D. diss., Pennsylvania State University, 2001.

Scully, Jackie Leach. "Drawing Lines, Crossing Lines: Ethics and the Challenge of Disabled Embodiment." *Feminist Theology* 11, no. 3 (2003): 265–80.

Spivey, Ted. *Flannery O'Connor: The Woman, the Thinker, the Visionary.* Macon, Ga.: Mercer University Press, 1997.

Swinton, John. "The Body of Christ Has Down's Syndrome: Theological Reflections on Vulnerability, Disability, and Graceful Communities." *Journal of Pastoral Theology* 13, no. 2 (2003): 66–78. Also available online at http://www.abdn.ac.uk/cshad/TheBodyofChristHasDownSyndrome.htm.

Thomas, Wendy. "More Instructive Than a Long Trip to Europe: The Effects of Lupus on Flannery O'Connor's Short Stories." Master's thesis, University of New Brunswick, 1997.

Thomson, Rosemarie Garland. *Extraordinary Bodies: Figuring Disability in American Culture and Literature.* New York: Columbia University Press, 1997.

Walls, Neal. "The Origins of the Disabled Body: Disability in Ancient Mesopotamia." In *This Abled Body: Rethinking Disabilities in Biblical Studies,* edited by Hector Avalos, Sarah Melcher, and Jeremy Schipper, 13–30. Atlanta: Society of Biblical Literature, 2007.

Watkins, Steven. "Teilhard de Chardin's View of Diminishment and the Late Stories of Flannery O'Connor." Ph.D. diss., University of Texas at Arlington, 2005.

Webber, Jay. "Better Off Dead?" *First Things* (May 2002): 10–12. Also available online at http://www.pregnantpause.org/court/wronlife.htm.

Weiss Block, Jennie. *Copious Hosting: A Theology of Access for People with Disabilities.* New York: Continuum, 2000.

Wood, Ralph. *The Comedy of Redemption: Christian Faith and Comic Vision in Four American Novelists.* Notre Dame: University of Notre Dame Press, 1988.

———. *Flannery O'Connor and the Christ-Haunted South.* Grand Rapids: Eerdmans, 2004.

———. "Sacramental Suffering: The Friendship of Flannery O'Connor and Elizabeth Hester." *Modern Theology* 24, no. 3 (2008): 387–411.

———. "The Scandalous Baptism of Harry Ashfield: Flannery O'Connor's 'The River.'" In *Inside the Church of Flannery O'Connor: Sacrament, Sacramental, and the Sacred in Her Fiction,* edited by Joanne Halleran McMullen and Jon Parrish Peede, 189–204. Macon, Ga.: Mercer University Press, 2007.

World Council of Churches. "A Church of All and For All: An Interim Statement." *International Review of Missions* 93, no. 370/371 (2004): 505–25. Also available online at http://www2.wcc-coe.org/ccdocuments2003.nsf/index/plen-1.1-en.html.

Yong, Amos. *Theology and Down Syndrome: Reimagining Disability in Late Modernity.* Waco, Tex.: Baylor University Press, 2007.

Index